Happiness Ruined Everything

First published by Galileo Press in 2025
Aiken, South Carolina

online at www.freegalileo.com

Book design by Adam Robinson
Cover photo by Shef Reynolds

HAPPINESS RUINED EVERYTHING

Michael Klein

Table of Devotions

Acknowledgements

Some of these essays appeared, at times in different form, in the following publications: *SPIN, Poetry, Slice, Poets & Writers, Ploughshares Blog, Tin House, Los Angeles Review of Books, & FENCE*

This book is for Beth Eisenberg

Introduction

> *Piglet sidled up to Pooh from behind.*
> *"Pooh!" .... he whispered.*
> *"Yes, Piglet?"*
> *"Nothing," said Piglet, taking Pooh's paw.*
> *"I just wanted to be sure of you."*

When I stopped drinking 40 years ago, I was told that as soon as I stopped throwing up I had better get a sponsor—someone who had been sober awhile and could act as my shepherd through a new mystery called sobriety. The word itself, *sobriety*, sounded something like grace. I had a lot of sponsors over the years and each one of them gave me something singular having to do with devotion—not to each other—but to the same idea. "Is this wisdom or self-pity? The love I have known is two people looking, not at each other, but in the same direction," wrote poet, Frank Bidart. I have known this kind of love, too.

Each sponsor I've had in the more than 20 years of sponsorship gave rise to a moment that could only be called transcendent—something they said or did was so tender, so sudden, and so generous as to be breathtaking.

Grace falls.

Steve was my first sponsor, and he had the distinction of being in a long-term relationship with a guy he paid for sex. Of course, the arrangement intrigued me—not the money part so much as the falling in love part. How did love happen? What hinge connects lust to love—when the hustler's eyes that had always been open during a kiss slowly begin to close?

Steve happened so long ago and only lasted one summer. I can't remember how we drifted apart, and I don't know if he is even still alive. I have been, shamefully, afraid to find out because he, like a lot of men I knew in the late '80s, had AIDS but was for the most part healthy, making plans based on living, not dying.

Once, in August of that year, Steve and a small group of us went to Riis Park, the iconic gay beach in New York. I set my towel down next to Steve's and we were lying on our stomachs talking about the book, *The Marriage of Cadmus and Harmony*, Roberto Calasso's visionary and encyclopedic retelling of Greek mythology. In the silence that followed our enthusiasm for the book, Steve touched my shoulder.

"What?" I said, waiting for his afterthought.

"Oh, no, nothing. I just wanted to keep in touch."

A few years later, another transcendent moment, when another sponsor, the beautiful, late Peter Baird, dropped everything he was doing to drive me from New York to Provincetown, because I didn't have a car anymore. The poet Jean Valentine, my closest friend at that time, had sold me her car for $1.00 (the car had no second gear), as a gift to get me out of New York. But the day before I was scheduled to leave, as I walked to where I parked the car in Riverside Park, holding the new license plates like an offering to the God of safe travel, I discovered the car had been stolen. I called Peter, and Peter was there the next day.

When we got to the Cape, the first thing we did was walk the length of Commercial Street to where it meets the breakwater and then across the breakwater in the dark because, as Peter said, "Night, when you can't see everything, gives you the soul of a place."

While those journeys with Peter and Steve were singular and indelible, most of the other people—my God Squad, as another sponsor once called it—were artists who, whether I knew them well or met them only once, have had a reverberating effect on my curiosity.

I watched how they lived.

I listened to what they said.

I shared in their successes.

Like someone who wants that ineffable something long-term sobriety promises, I wanted what artists had—artists who seemed to fall into my path through my education. And in that same moment, thinking about the God Squad, I realized I've never acknowledged those people in writing or what it was that made me wonder—not only about the world of making art, but what it was that I could offer that world, something that wasn't (I knew it wasn't) going to be children. The years of my training in acting, music, dance, and writing all culminated in my becoming someone who found the wonderment that comes with writing poems.

So, this is my book about what it has meant to me to stay curious and devoted to certain people, places, and things, and how they all helped set out on a path based not on logic, but on imagination.

Wonder is becoming a rare emotion

 —Charles Simic

Making Something

Most of the autobiographical writing I've done has focused on bringing to the surface dark episodes from a sad and chaotic past in my attempt to turn this pain into art. At least that's the way I was once characterized by the host of a reading I gave at the University of Wisconsin a lot of years ago. But even in that chaos, I see salvageable and sometimes extended moments of joy, having mostly to do with my restless curiosity about creativity.

While it may have appeared to anyone else that I was merely dabbling in the arts (except for poems, which I was always serious about, from the beginning) each new discipline represented another astonishment about a way of being. Each a road less travelled, not knowing that Robert Frost's line would become mine, too.

So, with my parents blessing (and they always blessed my curiosity, if nothing else), I attended acting classes from an early age at the venerable New York institutions American Academy of Dramatic Art and Neighborhood Playhouse. I then attended the High School of Music & Art, where I was a voice and composition major. And then, at Bennington College, I turned to dance and choreography because I wanted to have a dancer's body.

But there was always poetry, which to my great luck started by studying with Adrienne Rich, who was a mentor to me her entire life. Adrienne's son, David Conrad, had been a friend in junior high school, which coincided with my interest in and obsession with reading and writing poetry. My relationship to Adrienne was thus an organic one.

I'm 71 years old and have never felt my age and the weight of my past more than I do now. The poems don't come as quickly as they used to, though their power has gotten even stronger. Within the sacred light that falls on any road less traveled, there is the knowledge that there has to be something more to reality than only what I could make of it through my senses. I had a hunger, not for God, but for the phenomenal, and I leaned hard into creating a life centered around making something.

Women in childbirth create a new life while bearing the pain of labor, while what men seem to bear is *taking* life, in, what poet Amy Lowell names *a pattern called a war*. I got the idea from somewhere that living and dying includes giving something back to the mystery of being born. I'm not the kind of person who would ever thank my parents for giving me life, but I am grateful to them for the look and feel of life, even if I wanted to know the spirit side of it more—more than what happens to the body as it moves through time and disappears.

I wanted to make something that didn't include a child that grows up only to become a dead soldier—a book, or a play or poem or a dance—eventually trying my hand at them all. I considered painting, too, but didn't have the talent for it, beyond thinking there was something radical about smearing red paint on my lips and kissing a piece of poster-size paper in a 7th grade art class.

And I've never been able to draw what I'm looking at in a way that makes the act of looking—as it must feel for any painter—revelatory. I'm thinking here too much about being bad at drawing and missing the sort of electric pulse a visual artist must have, in the body, when seeing something—to *see* it in paint, or charcoal, or steel, or stone. But I've always loved the energetic silence I hear whenever I look at a painting—disappearing into that silence, as if the work was transporting me to the day the painter first envisioned what the painting could look like.

Thinking Poetry

There used to be a Yamaha grand piano in the basement of the music building at Goddard College that was always, strangely, in tune. Unusual—that in-tuneness—because, given the small population that was on campus at that time, I couldn't imagine the piano getting played much. I played it, though. The first thing I did when I got to Vermont to teach in the MFA program in the early '90s was go to that piano and fall into its, *his*, arms. And because he was a Yamaha with a tone less strident than the Steinways I've known; he was a great transmogrifyer. He made me sound better than I was.

I've always played by ear—even after years of music theory in high school. I play by ear because I have never been good at reading music. But I am a deep listener—committed to what I hear and then able to sing back complex phrases of music, part of the test you had to pass to get into the High School of Music & Art.

That sense of things—*knowing* music (but not knowing what it means when its written down), that pleasurable sleepwalking, allowed me to wander up and down the black-and-white boulevard of keys in a rapture. This was something I think only my self-education could evoke and made the piano more malleable to my touch when I forgot how I learned it. Improvisation was the only way I knew how to meet the keys and find the phrase of music that felt naturally next, because then I could remember which key made which sound based on where it was on the keyboard.

Writing happened the same way.

I never *formally* learned how to write. Before it became a vocation, I began the adventure of falling in and out of time through language with the feeling—broad as daylight—that I could only stay in the world by leaving it occasionally, as if I'd discovered a trapdoor to time. That secret knowledge also informed the way I saw the natural world, probably differently than how other people might see the same thing.

Trees are the go-to for this kind of thinking—i.e., trees didn't interest me nearly as much as their animation did—whatever it was that collaborated with a breeze to keep the leaves rustling. Not knowing *what else* was going on, except the air simply moving those leaves, also let me enter their poetry—the same way, I suspect, a person of faith enters a church.

As a kid, I read a lot of poetry because it was short. And there was a lot of it, right down the street from where I lived, at the Jefferson Market Library on Sixth Avenue between 9th & 10th Streets. In its previous life as a building, the library was the Women's House of Detention. The cacophony made by the incarcerated women yelling down to their friends and lovers on the street below filled the air of my childhood in the afternoons when school let out.

Poetry gave me something I knew instinctively, a knowledge that had nothing to do with the kind of thinking about it I'd eventually do the more I read it. It awoke in me a beauty I didn't find anywhere else—other than sometimes in plays—the beauty of language taken further than ordinary speech. Both kinds of writing gave me a treasure map to extraordinary people and ideas. Novels do this, too, of course, but I wasn't there yet, since what I was given to read in school was mostly very dull—the notable exception being *Johnny Got His Gun* by Dalton Trumbo.

I was impractical in my youth, and speech impaired. I was also a burgeoning addict, living with parents who were similarly caught between living and not knowing how to die. But reading and writing poems lit up my childhood, and my first moment of incorporeality came the day I couldn't sleep until I finished this:

> Weary people walk the streets.
> like shadows not quite real
> Where are they going, I wonder?
> Maybe to the harbor, to see the lonely ships.
> dark and misty like their own lost dreams.

It's a beginner's poem of course and heavy handed. Too much depends upon the metaphor. And please forgive my audacity for even including it as part of this devotional. But there's something there that doesn't resist a consciousness of difference—empathy for someone, or something, other than myself. That idea existed outside the realm of my experience at the time. I didn't identify with the weary people I wrote, per se, but I was engaged with who they seemed to be, inside a type of sadness that leads them down to the harbor.

I saw those people milling about. And it took years after following my own shadows down to the water, and only after I stopped drinking, that I got the courage to send work to magazines, leading eventually to getting published. And to get published was essential to me, if I was going to think of myself as a real writer, a real poet.

One day, drinking a cup of coffee at Lincoln Center with Jean Valentine, she casually mentioned that I might consider going for an MFA degree. And so, that summer, 1989, we drove up to Vermont to look at Vermont College because their low-residency model fit well with my working life. And if I could manage both, the working life would pay back the loan I'd need to attend in the first place.

Jean and I also traveled to Vermont to meet Mark Doty, because, at the time, I was also editing a book of poems about AIDS, and I'd been told that Mark had written a thrilling first book of poems on the subject—some of which I might consider for the anthology. As it happened, I included some of Mark's poems in the book, and I did end up going to Vermont College. From there, I went to Cape Cod in 1990, where I lived on a fellowship at the Fine Arts Work Center in Provincetown.

Having a fellowship and living in a town I had never been to turned out to be the single most important validation I ever got as a writer. Provincetown was more important to me than getting published or knowing if I could make any kind of living as a writer who was only writing poetry at the time.

In Provincetown I was broke most of the time. Because it wasn't my first time being broke, I already knew and had been charmed by the fact that having no money can put you in a state of nervous ecstasy. Rather than money, your labor gives back love. I was in love, too, with the cloudless, sunlit streaming of time where nothing was required of me. My only reminder of time came from a steeple bell at the Universalist Unitarian church in the center of town.

And, in that first winter of an alternate life, I fell in love with another person—a painter with red hair. I had forgotten about red hair and the boy I had a crush on so many years ago. I had, also, until I was now living at the edge of it, forgotten about the sea. The painter and the sea became a moving still-life, and I drove to the sea and let wind rock the car[1]. I kept thanking God for Provincetown and the man with red hair for being given seven months with nothing but my ideas, because they were all I could afford.

I lived in an apartment too far from the water to see the bay through the skylight, but I could hear the softness that distinguished the bay from the ocean. That sound, along with a foghorn striking its one mobius bass note, helped me write my first book of poems, which went on to be published by a press in town and from there to win an award. The award didn't give me any more success than I'd already had, which wasn't very much, but it didn't matter. I knew there was something very new, writing-wise, waiting for me after that first book of poetry.

In my second year of this ecstasy, I got a job in a restaurant so I could stay in Provincetown once the fellowship was over. I also started working on a memoir because the story I wanted to tell couldn't be told in poetry. I didn't know why that was so exactly, only that the poems I tried writing about the seven years when I worked on a racetrack, taking care of a horse who went on to win the Kentucky Derby, just weren't very good. They were way too lovey-dovey about horses. And while the memoir was going to be written in sentences that make paragraphs, I knew that poetry would have to be part of it too, somehow, because poetry was the diction I used to talk to the world.

I realized some time ago that I write nearly to the edge of resisting what I've written. I'm never satisfied. And in the process of putting my sentences together, a subject begins to emerge, one I hadn't begun with, like Nessie rising out of her Loch. I fight the monster; I acquiesce to the monster. I rewrite a scene and set a table for the monster. And then, in revision, writing takes me not where I wanted to go but where it wants me to go. There's no other way to say it that sounds less gooey than it is. The beauty part is that with each new draft, the writing keeps talking, taking over, more and more, knowing as it does how to make me disappear.

After a few hours of such disappearing, I get on the phone.

---

1 Reference to Adrienne Rich's "Like This Together," whose first line reads, "Wind rocks the car."

I've been away. I miss people.

Or I rent movies—classic black-and-white stories about outer space. Not the Martian outer space, but the existential outer spaciness that drifts dandelionly against the cosmos, fitting into the earthly sub-conscious—those vibrant spores streaming toward Earth in the classic film *Invasion of the Body Snatchers*. If you don't know the original (it was later made into a vastly different but equally scary-as-hell version in the '70s), it's a cinematic treatise on the effect individual thinking can have on a world that doesn't recognize the individual.

In the film, a town sleeps its way into conformity through easy duplication. Someone goes to bed the person they are and wakes up like everyone else—replaced by his or her deader version—a doppelganger, zombie-fied and with no feelings—vibrating on the same low frequency the rest of the world is tuned to.

The mission—one of its missions—of writing is, of course, to resist. Everything you thought you knew about the world must be resisted so the way you say something provides a reader with your take on that world. One way of resisting is to make a noise in your writing that rises above the dull tones of one-sentence-following-another—a mere telling of the story. There is nothing deadlier than the unrelenting rhythm of *and then what happened next*—words parceled out on a conveyor belt whose only job is to spit out bald information. Telling your story isn't enough. You must make a story live by igniting it and watching it burn.

One way to prevent this dullness of time is to put something into the work that is mysterious and *remains* mysterious—something the writer isn't compelled to explain away.

Explain, if you can, the extraordinary conclusion of Joyce's "The Dead." Or, more recently, the astounding last paragraph of Ann Patchett's memoir, *Truth and Beauty*, where she describes, as her own entry into epiphany, a Cocteau film she saw with the subject of her book, the late writer and Ann's best friend, Lucy Grealy. Explain some of the work of Clarice Lispector, William Gass, Jamaica Kincaid, John Ashbery, Annie Proulx, Sherwood Anderson. Explain (please *don't*, ever) Virginia Woolf's masterpiece, *The Waves*.

Wonder has become a rare emotion. And I sometimes see this as the identifying feature of someone in the throes of addiction or a mental health crisis. And the world now, being stuck in its low vibration—gives back a lot of *what is* rather than *what could be*. The latter is what art can do and does. I don't think it at all reductive or idealistic to declare that art, in all its devotions, as the thing that can save the world.

Because it is.

Because it has.

To be an artist doesn't require that you go out and accumulate death-defying experiences.. You don't even have to live an interesting life, just one that never stops resisting the easy, the unexamined, the force fed, the words coming from the mouths of desperate people in power. In these millennial years, you can challenge someone who still believes that war is an answer with this still radical idea: people were not born to kill each other.

Resist it all—everything—except your ability to be moved by the singularity of each one of us, of each of our lives—however joyful or horrible they may be.

Andre Dubus, the extraordinary writer who died at the end of 1998, wrote his most transporting work after a car accident put him in a wheelchair. What a bystander on the highway might have seen as someone's tragedy, Dubus saw as the work of an angel.

And Emily Dickinson didn't often open the front door to let in the outside world—a world she was mostly just thinking about. But that world and her ideas about that world never stopped moving through her because she received it as a locus for art. Her ideas were her experiences and gave her a life that wasn't linear, but circular—something I realized not from her poetry, but from what was written on her gravestone—a rubbing of which was the first thing I laid eyes on when I walked into Jean Valentine's living room for the first time:

Born: December 1830. Called back: May 1886.

Oliver, Fagin

In 1964 I am playing Oliver in the school play. My twin brother is playing Fagin.

Oliver is looking for his mother, for love, for someone to tell him his soul is wider than the abyss that overtakes the soul of an orphan.

Fagin is looking for money.

Actually, Oliver and Fagin are looking for the same thing—security.

But Oliver is the softer version, which feels closer to who I really am.

It is the role of a lifetime.

It is a role written around wonder and empathy and a certain naivete about the world, beyond the world of the orphanage.

Fagin is a tougher character—the mischievous thief, bathed in blue.

He is the adult looking for the child and Oliver is the child looking for the adult.

My brother plays Fagin the same way I would play Fagin: cranky, but with a sense of play.

My brother and I share an aesthetic. We like the same things, but we have different spins, different approaches, which my parents think they understand. The truth of how my parents saw us came through one Christmas when my brother got a little sports car to drive around in and I got a puppet theatre. Butch/Femme.

In the musical *Oliver!* I improvise—while my brother rests his arm on the banister of always knowing his lines—puppet sensibility versus car sensibility. My brother likes to know where he's supposed to be standing by the time he's finished singing a song called "Reviewing the Situation."

When I'm finished singing the song "Who Will Buy?" I might as well be floating in the clouds. I can never remember where I'm supposed to be standing. But the director doesn't mind. She's transfixed by directing twins. She's never worked with twins before. She thinks twins are trick dogs.

Acting feels like something my brother and I are naturally good at, which means we will never know how hard it is. We're undisciplined in that way. Inside us is something that floats—an aesthetic without craft. Dandelions. I forget whether dandelions are the yellow part or the part you blow away or if that's even the right flower or … isn't it a weed?

There's a scene where I've been adopted by an undertaker who I don't want to live with. I escape from his house and go through a window that opens into the backstage, which is where I live when I'm not acting.

In *Oliver!* my big songs are "I'd Do Anything" and "Where is Love?" Love is abstract, but I don't know that yet, the way I didn't know that Oliver and Fagin were looking for the same thing. I just know they're in the same play. Like me and my brother. Singing.

I think singing will bring people to me.

I think I will be discovered singing.

I think when they find me dead I will have just been singing.

I switch roles with my brother in a dream. We spend our childhood switching roles, switching classes, switching boyfriends and girlfriends. In the dream, I'm Fagin living in a den of beaming male youth. We are all living in a loft in Brooklyn. I send my graffiti artists out along the rail lines to mark up the city. This isn't Fagin's money dream. There isn't any money anymore.

I take the boys from their mothers because I love them more than any woman could. I know what they need. It isn't just physical. I tell them that my love will turn into money, in case they don't believe that love can change into anything.

In *Oliver!* I make asking for more sound like singing.

My brother makes "Pick a Pocket or Two" sound like an anthem.

We are good little actors. Singers. Troopers. On stage, off stage. School. On the way home. Home. Life behind life.

We're discontent. The actor is like the poet in that way. Discontent, no identity.

In a letter, Keats said that the poet has no identity. The poet is the most unpoetic creature in the world. The poet is anonymous.

In Order

E.L. Doctorow once taught a course at NYU with only one book on the syllabus. The class read the book and decided then what they wanted to read next. If the book was *Jane Eyre*, for instance, someone might suggest *The Wide Sargasso Sea*, the prequel written by another writer at a completely different time. Perhaps reading both books would give a reader a rounder sense of the created world when seen through the eyes of different characters. Or one could, by extension, if they were in an architecture class, read something about Gaudi that would lead them to a book set in Barcelona—Colm Toibin's *Homage to Barcelona*, for example.

I have no idea if Doctorow's class was a literature course or a writing workshop or if this story is even true, but it doesn't matter, it's the idea that counts, and it's a great one. What's so right about the idea is that it mirrors the way a deep reader is curious. A lot of us read like this anyway—at least we do when away from the academy. We read books in the order of our lives, or, more precisely, in the order of where our interest takes us.

When Jean and Adrienne were students at Radcliffe, the Dean of the school suggested they both take General Studies because, even though they were there to write poetry, poetry wasn't offered—not for credit, anyway. In a way, they lucked out. In General Studies, they had to read *everything*. Jean later told me how the course made her a better poet than if she had only read poetry. Randall Jarrell meant something similar when he said, "Read at whim."

When my friend Beth (an extraordinary pianist) and I applied to Bennington College, I asked her what attracted her to the school. Bennington was famously hard to get into, and neither of us had done very well in the complicated hormonal tempest that is high school. Beth's very matter-of-fact answer was, "I want to go there because I want to talk about Bach with an architecture major." Architecture, of course, could be considered a back road to Bach. Beth didn't necessarily want to talk about how the music made her feel (which is how we usually talk about music) but how the music was *built*—*in the same* way people talk about mathematics and music. My friend wanted to bring logic to something ephemeral.

Most writers I know are incredibly curious about how life is built—which brings them to so many subjects. This probably accounts for why I am always reading at least two or three books at once: a book or two of poetry and a book of non-fiction. And, if I'm feeling really adventurous, a novel as well. But a novel, for me, is the hardest thing to read. There's usually structure to a novel, and I like looser structure than most fiction delivers. I occasionally liken reading to dreaming—the way John Gardner talks about entering the world of fiction as you would a dream. Because I go back and forth with books, they begin to read into each other and put me in a zone like Alpha but not quite Alpha. This crowding of subjects starts to sound dissonant, but I like dissonance in music and art.

I am more of a cataloging listener than I am a reader, though. I generally listen to all the music by one person and then go on to some next singer or composer. I don't do that so much with books. I haven't read—I don't think—all the books by any living writer (principle before personality?) except all the books by certain poets. But even there, I'm particular, if I think a poet is just doing the same thing they did the last time and the time before that.

What to read next?

Maybe a book from any number of the stacks that surround me, which have always surrounded me—stacks arranged in the order of my curiosity. The newest books are usually on top. Even if I never get to all of them, the sight of those high-piled books is evidence of the only true republic for which we stand—our imagination.

Steve Paxton

I fell in love with the dancer and choreographer Steve Paxton the moment I laid eyes on him. I am trying to remember where that was exactly—which room, *which* outside—except I do know it was at Bennington College, where I was a student and Steve Paxton was on the faculty. And there I watched him dance.

I never saw anybody move with so much childlikeness—as though he had no other language to talk about beauty or where it came from except for how his body talked about that beauty. This was also the first time I remember thinking that beauty could be sexual—that you could touch with your body an idea of the world that had once been sacred.

My schoolboy crush never amounted to anything—anything sexual. But Paxton managed to soak up the attention I lavished upon him like a sponge—the way a lot of straight men thrive in the ambiguous glow of gay attention right up to the point where the muscle is asked to flex. So, it was a shock when I found out after leaving Bennington that Paxton was queer. And, of course, it was almost not knowing he was queer that fed my attraction—which is the same organizing principle of obsession—it's the kindling of not having, not knowing, that starts a fire. In my ongoing daze of love, mixed up with beauty mixed up with dance mixed up with ritual, I would leave him gifts in his mailbox.

One winter afternoon during our imaginary love life, I found Paxton's red truck in the parking lot and left him a Seals and Crofts album, which I slipped between the wiper and the windshield. Unlike many teachers at Bennington at that time—the '70s—he actually had boundaries and never returned any of my dozens of amorous gestures. But there were two extraordinary episodes with Paxton that I now see as acknowledgements of how I felt about him, which said, *Here, Michael. This I can give to you.*

Once, after a particularly rigorous improv class he was teaching in a building that had, strangely enough, shower stalls in the basement, Steve announced: *OK, everyone hit the showers*. Hoping against hope that I would get to see Steve naked—or even more spectacularly, that we would be naked together in the same water—I ran down the stairs, ripped off my clothes, and waited for the teacher to appear, the student was ready.

Of course, Steve never came downstairs. Nobody came downstairs, and there I was: stalled and self-conscious. I suddenly saw the stairs in my mind as the longest in the world, leading to the most dark and awful place beneath the earth. I was embarrassed to be so full of what I thought was love and to stand there naked and alone with it. It was the first time I sensed a danger around my heart—the first electrical shock that could lead to a life of ruin.

The other gift I got from Paxton was the very heat of his dancing.

I was a strange and ritualistic kind of college student, due in part to the sad concoction of alcohol rigorously shaken and mixed with a lonely mind floating in vague expectation. For the first few weeks into spring, whenever the sun was going down, I would go up to the dance studio where there was a particularly funky piano (I liked pianos that produced a sound resembling tiny hammers hitting tin) and sit down and improvise. A piano eats my mind, and in one of those improvisatory spells that lasted an hour or so, Paxton entered the room and began to dance. He liked to dance to Bach in those days, but the music playing in that Bennington dance studio, circa 1973, while the sun fell away from the world, was something only I could have made up.

Piano Music

The Bushes was this cheery little dump of a place at the back of the huge lobby of an apartment building (or was it a hotel?) off Central Park West. It wasn't a top-tier room, but it wasn't completely unknown either. Somewhat like Brothers and Sisters on 46th Street—a lot of Broadway performers would rush up to 73rd Street and perform in showcases at The Bushes after the curtain in the musicals they were in came down. I never thought I'd succeed as a cabaret artist; I was just too outside the box. Singing always felt like a bridge to something else—poetry, as it turned out.

The good memory about that night at The Bushes was that I was performing my own stuff while the brilliant jazz pianist Mike Renzi sat at the bar, and after playing my first song, he yelled out, "really interesting chords!"

Life is a cabaret.

Cabaret

(Broadway, Broadhurst Theatre, 1969)

After we saw *Cabaret*, we all took the bus up Central Park West with cast members Bert Convy and Joel Grey. Joel Grey lived in our building and gave us the tickets to see him in a musical I imagined was about how good Germans were in bed and what good spies they were, too. I couldn't separate the spying from the sex when I heard "It Couldn't Please Me More (The Pineapple Song)" or "So What?," which is one of the most beautiful songs I've ever heard written for the theater. It's a song of onomatopoeia. It sounds exactly like what it's about—impatience mixed with a raw longing for the past..

> "So, the sun will rise
> and the moon will set
> and you learn how to settle for what you get
> it will all go on if we're here or not
> So who cares? So, what."

Then, Lotte Lenya tells a story about living by the sea, which is how she became of the mind to say *so what*. Lotte Lenya has the most beautiful broken voice I ever heard. Lotte Lenya's voice that sounds like it rights itself by singing.

There is no simple formula for the relationship of art to justice. But I do know that art—in my own case the art of poetry—means nothing if it simply decorates the dinner table of power which holds it hostage.

—Adrienne Rich

Stephen Sondheim

I once sponsored another recovering alcoholic who ended up sponsoring me. His name was Bob, and he was the house manager at a theater in Brooklyn. Before that, he had been a sheriff in a small town in the middle of America. I asked Bob to sponsor me because he knew more about how to be in a relationship than I did, and I was yearning to be in a relationship with somebody. I was sober, goddamn it. Bring on the men!

But I wasn't sober enough to get people to tell me more about themselves, or how to ask, or how to behave on a date. I never practiced how much to reveal about who I was and how much to keep a mystery. The only time I have ever been mysterious was when I combined too many drugs at a theater legend's New Year's Eve party in the late '80s and was thrown out into the snowstorm.

Whenever I was in lust with someone in the early years of not drinking, it never went further than the crush. Something in me—and this, after an 11-year relationship—resisted anything that might bring a couple into continuity. I would get crushes on guys who were newly sober. And whenever that would happen, Bob S. would ask "Have you given them the Sondheim tapes?" (His way—I caught on immediately—of gauging the seriousness of the crush and thus premeasure the extent of the aftershock of being crushed by the crush.)

What my new sponsor was referring to was that dizzying moment of triumph in which—because these crushes were always on men too young to know who Stephen Sondheim was—it as my mission to turn these beautiful boys into beautiful theater queens. They would then thank me in the eternity of their Sondheimian bliss, where I would appear to them like a gravel-sounding angel whenever a Sondheim song was in the air. I loved being Stephen Sondheim's go-between (though I strongly suspected—no, I *knew*—that as gay men, we were already legion). It's true what homophobes have always said about us—we do recruit. Not boys into queers, but men into an army of Sondheim-ites.

Still, with all that unconditional music playing in the swooning heads of these new recruits, it was a non-recruit, my own twin brother, Kevin, who had an actual personal connection to Sondheim through a correspondence that lasted for years—as seen in the letters I inherited after my brother's death—letters my brother never told me about until the year before he died, alone, in a Boston SRO. Letters that now live in what is left of a 50-year-old wicker suitcase Kevin liked the look of, but never used, because it was falling apart.

The correspondence between my brother and the world-renowned composer had started the way so many of these things do—as a note from a fan—which the fan sees as a love letter and the recipient sees as too much of a bother to take on. The thing was, Sondheim's generosity was legendary, and Kevin was particularly good at writing letters—a poet who wrote letters, not a letter writer.

STEPHEN SONDHEIM

January 4, 1990

Dear Kevin -

The poem is very touching, and one of your best, I think. But then I like short lines.

Assassins is terrific. It leaves everybody, as one of them put it, feeling as if they've been run over by an express train.

I don't plan to retire on the proceeds.

As ever,

Sondheim was intrigued by my brother and his writing and sent him CDs, and comps to *Sunday in the Park with George* and *Into the Woods*. And—through the letters and phone calls my brother would get from Sondheim when he was working in a store that sold all things lighting—Sondheim would gossip, an essential aspect of every interview he's ever given.

It always has seemed to me that Sondheim was magnetically, almost combustibly—enthralled with being alive, through his specific curiosity about other people—those characters he wrote songs for. I always looked for his childlike, mischievous grin whenever he appeared in public—being interviewed or honored—a grin that announced his rightful knowledge that nobody was smarter than he was. And it was precisely his curiosity that fostered his lifelong interest in what younger artists were doing.

When Sondheim singled out Laura Nyro from that generation of singer-songwriters to praise, it made me respect and love him even more, as Nyro has always been my obsession. As for other kinds of music written in his lifetime, like rock, Sondheim wasn't a fan. Rock was a genre of music, a teacher of mine once said, that came from musicians who are paid to learn how to play music. But later on, Sondheim came to admire Steve Reich and Radiohead and Jonny Greenwood.

Once, Sondheim helped my brother get a poem published in *The Yale Review*, where his friend, J.D. McClatchy, was the poetry editor. And when my brother and the composer finally met in New York and spent some hours in conversation, there were two stories Kevin told me that were pretty remarkable—one about Barbara Streisand and one about Madonna.

When Streisand was making *The Broadway Album*, she and Sondheim would talk on the phone, and she later told him she'd been recording their conversations for—her word: *posterity*. At that, apparently, he never spoke to her again.

And when Madonna and Sondheim were in the studio recording the songs from the movie, *Dick Tracy*, something blew on the soundboard, and they had to stop and wait for whatever it was to be fixed. While she was waiting to sing again, Madonna tapped her fingers on the piano and impatiently said, "All I want to do is make my money," to which the maestro uttered one word: "Impossible."

And then, there's a story about Dean Jones wanting to leave the cast of *Company* and, drunk at a party attended by Sondheim said, "Who do you have to fuck to get out of this show?" And Sondheim yelling back, "The same person you fucked to get in it."

My only correspondence with Sondheim happened when I was putting *Poets for Life: 76 Poets Respond to AIDS* together and I wrote him a letter asking if he would consider writing something. His letter back said something to the effect of, I don't know anything about writing a poem, which, of course, I took as false modesty. But he was actually telling the truth. Sondheim never considered his lyrics to be anything more than words written for a musical—always revealing in a lyric the longing inherent to both character and plot. Plot—I would venture to say—because every plot is a puzzle, and Sondheim was devoted to the puzzle making as the a dependable and surprising way to organize a musical.

The puzzle of a lyric itself is that it only happens once, whereas a poem, he was always fond of saying, has to be read twice.

Still .... take lines like:
take me to the world, so I can be alive.
every day, a little death.
Pretty women, blowing out their candles, or combing out their hair, even when they leave, they still are there. They're there.

Or the existential:
if it happened, I was there,
There won't be trumpets
I know how soon a dream becomes an expectation
alone is alone, not alive.

His producer for most of the original cast albums was Thomas Z. Shepard, who was a client at the law firm where I was working and said the most beautiful thing one afternoon while he was waiting in the conference room.

"I hear music all the time. I'm hearing it now."

I don't know what to do with my brother's suitcase of magic letters because they're not, in a strange way, enough to mean anything beyond their ongoing generosity—lights on a path my brother needed because he'd hoped the lights would never go out.

The letters sit in their easy willingness to greet another person—not saying very much about Sondheim, not saying very much about my brother. But it doesn't matter. The value of the correspondence is that they're evidence of some grace at a time when a letter—sometimes a letter from anybody to anybody—meant that, in your one life, you were alive in somebody else's.

Not a day goes by, not a single day, in the last 50 years, that something of Sondheim's hasn't been playing in my head.

I hear him all the time.

I'm hearing him now.

Laura Nyro

In 1968, there was a record store on 85th Street and Broadway where I went every other Saturday to search through the new releases. For me, this store, along with bookstores, were the keys to the kingdom and browsing was one of the great acts of imagination. This pull toward music began an obsessive interest in me for the singer-songwriter—that rare artist— troubadour, really—who signs off on something they created, without asking for any money upfront—the way the music business seems to be run today.

On one of those Saturdays, I came across an album called *Eli and the Thirteenth Confession* by someone named Laura Nyro—an excitingly odd-titled new release that came wrapped in a lavender lyric sheet treated with a fragrance I think was honeysuckle.

"Who's Laura Nyro," I asked the shopkeeper, a serious music lover who made it a point to listen to every new album the day it got to the store.

"Never heard of her," he said, not yet having gotten to *Eli*...

But it didn't matter. I loved the package and the title and the lavender lyric sheet and brought that Saturday's singer-songwriter home with me—spending the next week, month, entire winter, devouring *Eli and the Thirteenth Confession*, which entailed—because every devotion requires some imitation—memorizing the lyrics and sounding out the songs on the piano.

The first time I put Laura Nyro's album on the gray plastic turntable of a cheap plastic record player (a toy with a plug), there wasn't enough time to hear everything the music was doing. I had to play the record every day for a week and more to learn how to listen to it. Nyro's songs, other than those that became hits for other people, are richly unclassifiable—meshing pop, gospel, and even 20th-century music influences—delivered by a singing voice with a three-octave range that seems to unfold with the urgency of confession. As a burgeoning singer-songwriter myself who was also drawn to the autobiographical, I wanted her music to seep into my DNA.

Eli and the Thirteenth Confession was released in 1968, the year before Woodstock and Manson, when everyone I knew considered listening to music an actual activity, not merely something lingering in the background while everyone was busy doing something else—something to forget there was music.

Classical music, as I learned in high school, teaches you how to listen. Jazz taught me this, too.

I'm sitting on the bedroom floor memorizing—no, *capturing*—every note of music and line of lyric. *Eli and the Thirteenth Confession*, and Nyro's next album—*New York Tendaberry*—made me feel something sensual but unrecognizable, like walking into the sunset after your first sexual encounter. *New York Tendaberry* is as soulful and original as her previous recording, but while *Eli...* had me thinking of Motown by way of show music, *New York Tendaberry* took me to Aaron Copland, another context for structure—a narrative you hear in classical song cycles.

The day Laura Nyro died, April of 1997, I was teaching at Sarah Lawrence and picked up a copy of *The New York Times* to read on the train ride home to Manhattan. I never bought the *Times*, and it seemed mystical to me that the one day I did, Laura Nyro's obituary would appear. Her cause of death at 49 was ovarian cancer, the same cancer that killed her mother—also at age 49. The obituary shocked me, the way the death of any idol pricks at the devotion that lives in the psyche. But it wasn't just the death of a beloved musician I was feeling, but the death of an *influence*. I felt as though the joy from hearing her music for the first time had now been relegated to sadness, knowing there would be no more of it.

The day after she died, I wrote a short devotional to her and her music and gave it to an agent to try and get placed somewhere. He liked it enough to send it over to a young editor at *The New Yorker*. After circulating it around the magazine for comments, someone got back to the agent a few days later and said, "I'm sorry, no one here ever heard of Laura Nyro."

Of course, her songs live on—something we say so much that the sentiment has lost its gratefulness. But when certain musicians die and that specific music made from their life stops being invented, it feels like a scar, or a ripple on the elusive nature of time. Laura Nyro's passing was a reminder that music is even more necessary in life because it is ephemeral—which, as it happens, is the way of the artist's life, too.

Did I Ever Really Live?

Like every great singer, Dawn Hampton's cabaret repertoire consisted, in part, of songs most people were hearing for the first time. One of those songs was "Did I Ever Really Live" by Allen Sherman and Albert Hague. It's a song from a failed musical called *The Fig Leaves are Falling*—the awful title alone almost assuring the musical's demise. It's a list song that runs through the ages of life: *you're born, you weep, you smile, you sleep, you cling, you crawl, you stand, you fall,* but neglects, through a kind of naiveté built into the progression, to put love on the list. And without love on the list, the song hauntingly asks at the end, *did I ever really live?*

I hear that song in my head every week or so—almost as much as I hear, lately, Adam Guettel's song "Fable" from the musical, *Light in the Piazza.*

I also hear junk, but that's not important. Junk gets in between one song and another.

While there's some stuff on YouTube, the only physical recording of Dawn Hampton I could find was on an original cast album of an off-Broadway revue called *Greenwich Village U.S.A.,* with an Unexpurgated! banner on the cover. But there is also a wonderful rendition of "Did I Ever Really Live," recorded by Mark Murphy, that I've been listening to lately, and there's also a strange (but worth looking at) rendition by Pat Paulsen that aired on the old *Smothers Brothers* TV show. Paulsen kind of clobbers the song because the serious eyes of this otherwise very funny performer don't know how to look into the camera. The song still delivers because it's that good and that powerful—a song that could easily have borrowed anybody.

I liked "Did I Ever Really Live" most when it borrowed Dawn Hampton's body.

Overture without Music

"If you want to screw around, just don't tell me about it."

I bored myself saying it. It was such a cliché.

But why not tell each other about it?

What kind of trust is there in a relationship where two people are secretly screwing around on each other? If I came home one day and said, "I just had the best fuck of my life," would that end the relationship? People break up over this all the time and when they are frozen in the act of finding out, it stuns the heart. It makes you seem like a single person again—turning back time to when you were bemoaning you weren't in a relationship.

Not wanting to know your partner is screwing around is precisely why it *isn't* an open relationship, but a relationship based on an inability to trust each other. Not wanting to know means that the other person isn't willing to tell, either. Are you in a secret relationship with each other?

That same secret energy, ironically, is exactly what makes anonymous sex so exciting. You and your 24-hour lover both know it's *because* of the sex that you never have to see each other again. The orgasm you each have with each other feels immortal because it's the only one you will have with each other. My subscription to anonymous sex expired years ago. And besides all that, I'm a throwback, a sexual homebody. I fall in love with someone and end up staying—resisting the popular gay paradigm that every man is a predator made for multiple sex partners. More than once, I have had a paradoxical conversation with a man about being in an open relationship that nonetheless concludes, "But I always come home to my honey every night."

A few years ago, I had lunch with a man half my age who was about to come out with his first book of poems. He asked me as soon as I sat down if I was in an open relationship—an essential compass needed to locate my house on the map of homosexual country. His question startled me, and I thought he was trying impress me with his ballsiness, and I would say nerve—which, in that first book of his poetry, he presented in poem after poem about sex.

"No," I told him. "I don't really believe in open relationships. I think they're escapist. I think it's like bisexuality—another form of non-commitment." Whether I actually believe that I'm not sure, but I was on a roll.

"More importantly," I told him, "I'm just not wired that way. I've always been monogamous. I've had two long-term relationships in my life—screwed around maybe twice, at a gym—but nothing like enough sex outside the main relationship for it to become anything like acceptable."

My poet friend was flabbergasted. Not only did he inform me that I was in the shallow minority of queers that he knew, but that there was something sort of unhealthy about me, that I wasn't making evolutionary strides as an American homosexual, that I hadn't kept up with the accepted mores about hooking up, unhooking up, and going home. I wasn't merely sexually undesirable; I was sexually undetectable.

◻

I used to live on the edge of the sea in a cottage that sat on the Provincetown/Truro line, where you could take the beach route all the way to the center of town. One year, many summers ago, I arranged to meet a man halfway between my cottage and the town to give him a copy of one of my just published books because he didn't know I was a writer. All he knew was that he liked the sound of my voice and thought I was funny. The beach that day was empty, and the tide was slowly coming in. The slowness of the clouds pulling away from the faint blue underneath made the sky look like it was unmaking a bed.

We met for the first time a few years before at a book fair. He was a painter who just split up with a writer, who, in the painter's words, was so quiet that he forgot who the painter was, with days going by when the painter couldn't remember the last thing the writer said to him. He told me they were in an open relationship, that casual sex with other people was something they knew about each other. But that's not what ended the relationship. What ended it was the writer's secrecy and how that secrecy made him curl up into a ball so small as to make him invisible, until in the end the painter couldn't find the writer.

And then, one day, the painter stopped looking.

He stopped caring.

He didn't love the writer anymore.

And then the writer disappeared.

What was strange for me, was that the painter stirred up romantic feelings that I hadn't felt since I'd met my husband. And it was confusing. But I found myself welcoming the feelings in their quiet but sparkling oddness, which made me feel modest, too.

The pot we smoked together might have caused those welcoming feelings, or the modesty that came just after, so I didn't feel shame when I didn't want to push the painter away—when, passing the joint, the hairs on his arm brushed against the hairs on mine. I wanted our arms to stay touching.

We were watching a video on his cell phone.

He was singing in a production of a musical in the town where he lives. *Pippin*? I can't remember because the touch of his arm against mine electrified me. And there I was, inhabiting a space where we knew each other, almost swooning in the brief lifetime of it.

A few days after the beach, I typed this and sent it through the air: *You know, I meant to tell you that the night in Provincetown with you was one of the nicest I have had with another person in a long time. Without sounding gushy, it was almost romantic.*

His arrow back: *Don't go getting sweet on me.*

And then, for a long time, I didn't hear from him.

But I've been thinking—maybe this is the kind of open relationship I could actually bear or at least manage—the one that ends before it begins. It's not sad, it's not hopeful, but it's still like a jewel. You meet a man, you walk in the dark, you see him again in the light of day or the barely-yet-light.

You meet him halfway, with the book you wrote to give to him, which is way more exciting because he didn't know you were a writer.

You send him a text.

You make a connection, and then you stop at the signal stage.

It was an overture without music.

And nobody got hurt.

And you never told your husband about it.

And if you did, your husband—rational husband that he is—would have seen it simplistically—a story about meeting a man on a beach between here and the center of town.

But in this story, here is everywhere.

And my husband's version of it would have been right.

And then both of you would have known the beginning of the same story.

Except yours is still being written. And his story—rational husband, still—is long forgotten by now.

Three Andrews

1.

It never occurred to me that it may have been a mistake letting Andrew read the memoir I had written about the racetrack before laying eyes on me, but doing so turned out to be a gift—as confirmed by these words he said after finishing the book:

You know that part where you're watching your horse win the Derby and you say that sometimes it's best to be alone when experiencing some of life's greatest moments? I don't agree with that. I think the great moments are even better when you're with someone.

And what startled me about what he said was not the independence of his thought (which, of course, I admired, because it was smart), but how he managed to find a place in the book to insinuate himself: *I wish I was with you when that happened.*

So this is the beginning of love.

2.

I had to go to the emergency room last night. Some weird upper stomach spasm, or I was getting a hernia, or something that never happened to my body was happening to my body.

The person who did my intake said there were 14 people ahead of me to see the doctor. It was 11:48 p.m. and I was tired and wanted to go home. It's strange how you can remember a certain time, in a certain place—a place where you have never been before. A certain time: 11:48, exactly.

My stomach wasn't doing anything strange anymore so I left with Andrew and took a gypsy cab down the 10 blocks back to where we lived.

At one point, during that whatever-this-is, Andrew said it was like somebody was sticking a pin into my voodoo doll. And it did feel like that. Still, I didn't think it was funny: Andrew imagining me as a doll held in the air. I wanted support in that rough draft of something-happening, but because he was a funny guy, I got something else.

I wanted to judge him for this but I realized we don't have any right to custom order our comfort.

I wanted him to take my pain away, or make me think of something else, but instead he put his hand on the pain to listen to it, just as I was listening to it.

3.

I love to lie in bed and watch TV late at night and sometimes I remember lying unhappily in the unhappy hospital having my unhappy appendix out. I was a kid and my stepfather (in an uncharacteristic spasm of generosity) rented a television for my room. The television was so high in the corner that when it was off I imagined it was filming me moving in my dreams.

What happens with the television now is that I lie with Andrew and he goes to sleep and I go back and forth from watching whatever show I am watching to pushing on Andrew so he'll stop snoring.

It used to make me lonely: him, the beloved, falling away and me still very awake, involved in a story, the guest host of an old movie— moving through a time projected from a screen, finding something there that will make me unthink softly, soft into sleep. Though now it's no longer lonely, it's pleasurable: my little world of shows in the dark.

Attending to real life every now and then to watch Andrew sleep.

It is such a distinct departure from the self to watch somebody sleep that it feels nearly religious. When this happens, Andrew finishes entering my mind.

Image Results for the Sky

1.

Last night's dream opened with me and Andrew lying in an inflatable boat on some body of water somewhere in summer. A plane was slowly falling out of the sky and heading right towards us. I remember thinking in the dream, when thinking feels like you're pulling the length of a telescope further out, that I'd seen this before: a plane falling, floating almost, towards these two men in this boat. Then it stopped and Andrew knew instinctively nothing was going to happen to us.

Later that same day or year of the dream, I am in a house with a lot of people hanging around—all age groups; a house with a porch in the country and the air is very still. It's night and a young man is reading me a poem he wrote and asks me what I think of it and I secretly hate it but of course I don't tell him that.

I tell him it feels like the beginning of a poem.

I tell him there's no ghost poem and that every poem has a ghost poem—which upon waking, is an idea I don't know whether is true or not.

I'm reading a book by Charles Baxter about subtext, and the ghost idea, I'm sure, came out of there.

Suddenly, in the night of the dream the sky starts an incredible light show—kaleidoscopic, frightening—all about reminding the town enthralled below that the sky is a screen for the world without a projector. It tells us what it wants to tell us.

And then someone else reads a poem again, which is a better poem than the first poem.

2.

We're at the beach. Everybody is at the beach. It's summer, the beginning of summer—that light all mixed in with vapor. And Jean is there and me and Andrew and a slew of beautiful boys—beautiful the way they were at the beginning of liberation when all the queers looked like hippies.

And there's a car (there's always a car) and the guy I'm with (there's always a guy) is driving the other way—actually sitting the other way around—looking at where we were instead of where we're going. Miraculously, we get there—the part of the dream that feels goal oriented. But I don't know what we're there for exactly, unless it's for sex, which, in a lot of dreams—my dreams anyway—it is.

There's a carnival on the dream beach. In the rooms that border the beach women are painting floors and making flags and nobody (suddenly in the middle of the dream) is there that I know, and my cell phone (which the dream has decided to make into an old sneaker) splits in half and I'm thinking that Andrew will do everything he can to find me or at least take me somewhere where I can get another phone. But where we are, where I am in my dream, makes it very clear that, even though there are houses and the natural world at the intersection of so many people talking and being in so much summer, there is nothing like money or goods. There is as there always has been what we have made and what we brought with us. There is only what we can carry.

I'm doing a reading that night and so is Jean but in different places and I don't know how to reach her or Andrew or the vague choir of boys swimming in my mind or why I even need to reach this vague choir except for another fix of beauty. And I'm suddenly thinking mundanely (the way a schedule feels mundane and sharp in a dream), who will I have dinner with?

And so I start walking, broken sneaker in hand, down a street of trees, trees, the first trees all day, their first appearance in the dream. And I see a woman dressed for a performance of some kind because she is carrying a trumpet in a leather case and is dressed in that way musicians who play classical music get dressed—between inspired and formal, black and usually with sneakers.

And I say, "I know you."

And she says, "I know you."

And then she says, "Lisa Epstein, Music & Art."

And I say, "That's right."

And then I say, "Michael Klein."

And I wake up to Saturday's unexpected sunlight (it was supposed to be shitty today) into Andrew, into the world I always leave to go dream walking and I tell him about my dream and how sad I was that I didn't know where he was.

Andrew looked at me in this life with his eyes closed and said, "I was there." And then, with that *Grapes of Wrath* intention, "I was there behind the tree." Andrew said (*I will always be there, behind the tree, looking out for you.*)

Jean Valentine

To a Young Poet
for Michael Klein

This January night at ten below I wish you
true desire, like a rose: to stand
in your chest. Veined. Bloom.

Let you be. Reflected in the train window,
inside a thousand circles of public darkness,
desire, a round red star.

And desire again, a foliating wand,
and you the Jack of Wands.

The round red rose of sleep in bloom. This is
true desire, it lets you be.
It says, "No money here."

What does it taste like?
True desire. Eye-
shadow, cinnamon.

I don't think I ever read this poem that Jean dedicated to me until it appeared in one of her books—and even then, it never came up in our conversations—giving it an anonymous quality.

Once in a while, and in celebration of nothing in particular, Jean would ask me to close my eyes and she would place a gift in my open hand: every time, a variation on the same theme—the earth, in miniature. Her first gift was a wooden marble with tiny continents handpainted in green. Her next, the planet carefully etched with glitter, a Christmas ornament. There are six or seven of these worlds that I have held in my hands over the years, thanks to Jean.

But the last gift she gave me before she died in 2020 wasn't the world, it was a small wooden horse on wheels. Small worlds must have been harder to find that month, or it could have been Jean's deteriorating memory that made it hard for her to remember the theme to her giving. And it threw me at first—the horse not being another world—but perhaps the horse represented something that reminded Jean of my once-disheveled life—all those years ago when I lived on the racetrack.

While Jean's gifts told me a lot about who she was, there were other times with Jean that transcended anything I knew about her—arriving usually in the form of something she said in ordinary conversation. She was one of the few poets I've ever known who could sound, in everyday speech, like poetry—which sounds pretentious, but Jean was never pretentious.

Once, at a Quaker meetinghouse in Brooklyn, where we were giving a reading from an anthology of poems I'd just published about the early days of the AIDS crisis, Jean and I were looking at the crescent moon through a window on the staircase landing. She said, "It's shaped like that to keep luck from spilling out."

Another time, one August, as we walked down Pearl Street in Provincetown towards the bay, shining in the middle distance, she said, "Everything's sad except what's real."

Occasionally, she could be disarmingly funny. In Provincetown, again, during a weekend called "Fantasia Fair," when transvestites and sometimes their wives come to town for an annual convention, Jean said, "Do you think people will think I'm a man?"

Over the many years of our friendship, my gifts to Jean were less metaphorical than hers, usually practical, something she needed. One winter I bought her a new television with a video player after the one she had conked out. She was surprised to receive such an extravagant gift, especially from the likes of me, who was broke most of the time. A week or two later, Jean called—her voice in the key of panic.

"Mikey, I love it, but everything's in black and white."

"What do you mean black and white?"

"Even the movies that were made in color are coming through in black and white." To which I joked, in all seriousness, "Of course, they're in black and white, Jeanie, the movies know that it's you, the dream barker, the poet, sitting in the viewing booth."

When I went to Jean's to see what was happening with the TV, she slipped a video of *Singing in the Rain* into the mouth of the haunted contraption. I don't know if the musical was any better in black and white, but Jean seemed to like it just the same.

"It looks like a news report in the form of a musical," she said.

A writer is somebody for whom writing is more difficult than it is for other people.

—*Thomas Mann*

Blown By Bob

On August 18th, 1991, Hurricane Bob hit Provincetown hard enough for a T-shirt to be made about it: *I was blown by Bob*. I watched most of the storm through the window at Gabe's house—an intermittently shaking house that sat on the high point of the town—reading Patricia Bosworth's extraordinary biography of Diane Arbus and thinking about the time I met the photographer and knew, even then, still standing outside her oncoming fame, that she was utterly unique. Arbus had just received in the mail a pair of "X-ray" glasses—the kind you sent away for using a coupon from the back of a comic book. The glasses were supposed to give you X-ray vision, and she was looking *through* her hand as she held it up in front of a table lamp.

As turbulent as it was outside that day, it was also perfect napping weather—or weather for construction paper, scissors, and glue, or for soup. Before the storm, Gabe cut the sunflowers from his picture-perfect garden and set them on the kitchen table. The brilliant stalks were longer than the vase they were standing in, and watching Gabe with the sunflowers, I realized how I've always envied men who can navigate those parts of being alive that *only* have to do with knowing how to finish something—daily rituals that keep the ego out: baking, planting seeds, raising rabbits, herding cows, making furniture.

I lived with an architect once who took my breath away as I watched him take down a wall.

Occasionally, Gabe and I ran outside to feel the storm against our skin, to be in something like that—an act of God—to feel that act pushing on our minds. The sky had grown so colorless that we were in outer space, even more than usual. On any other day, there wouldn't be anything in the sky to show us we were moving at all—except a cloud or two, or a slow-moving train of clouds. But on that day, TV antennae were sailing through the air and roofs were flying and boats out in the bay were going under. And then it was a storm that seemed to have a distinct target in mind: the trees.

In the front lawn, limbs and leaves got mixed up with the fence. A telephone pole at the end of Pearl Street fell into a powerline, which suspended its crash and kept it from going through a roof. So many leaves were smashed onto the fronts of houses and their windows or were plastered onto cars that the streets looked camouflaged. And the sound of it all—this puffing and sucking—the sounds of impatience and centrifugal force.

The most spectacular thing I saw was in front of the historic 1807 house in the West End. A huge elm had uprooted, along with half the right side of the lawn. The wind pulled the roots up four or five feet, so that the hedges were turned nearly vertical.

In the week after the hurricane, the sound of wind and rain was replaced by the sound of generators and people clapping whenever a Com Electric truck would roll by on its way to restore power to so many houses. The light finally came back on in the studio where I lived, situated in the back of one of the only houses in Provincetown with two chimneys. One chimney went with a falling elm and the other a few days later when, in a tree-cutting mishap, a huge limb swung out of control and knocked the chimney over, slicing as it went through three Georgian columns on the house across the street.

The tree company didn't come back until the next morning to finish cutting the rest of the tree down. Then they sliced it in tire-sized sections and stacked them in the garden at my front door. Jackson Lambert, married to Carmen, owner of the property, restacked the tree sections late in the afternoon, so it resembled some variation of the original—his memorial to the savage beauty of hurricanes, I suppose.

At the front of the house, Carmen left her own memorial: a pink rose in a glass jar that sat on top of the three-foot stump—all that was left of the tree that had given the house so much of its shade. It was mild that day, and the wind wasn't strong enough to spin the rose around.

Bobby

Years of yesterdays ago, J.T. and I were talking about romance.

I know J.T. because of some radar we share. We're connected by inappropriateness. Sometimes we fall in love with friends.

Bobby was a friend I fell in love with once.

I fell in love with Bobby in the middle of a New Year's Day kiss.

We drove to a beach in Truro.

Thomas Merton said Truro sounds like a word that means the loneliness at the edge of the sea. I understood Merton's sentence so fast the day I kissed Bobby because that kiss was one stage away from loneliness and one stage toward loneliness—like the loneliness of being drunk.

Bobby's kiss was proof for what had been in the air for about a year. His kiss happened after it was in the air for so long with the light and the damp from the sea.

I fell for Bobby in a room next to the sea. And I watched him, as he wandered into an AA meeting. He looked like the painting of the young priest hanging on the wall in the middle of the room. The priest was beautiful, but a little haunted, like he had seen the wrong death—that the death he saw would not let his life fit into it.

Bobby looked broken-spirited, too. He was a rumpled and beautiful character out of a Dostoyevsky novel—Rogozin, *The Idiot*.

It was winter, so Bobby was bundled, and then his heavy gray wool overcoat gave way to a T-shirt and shorts. He was lean and Mediterranean handsome and looked like summer—which means that since it was winter, he was someone dressed for a dream.

I was drawn to Bobby. Badly.

An obsession was percolating, which meant that I was making Bobby up as we went along just as much as I was trying to figure out who Bobby actually was. I was attracted to what drew Bobby in: the sea and the men and women huddled around the coffeemaker pockmarked with dents.

I was thinking, while standing there with the drunks, that I have always been drawn to men who don't dress for the weather—men who are in the world but not wholly of the world. Dreamers. The job of the world, where the dreamer is concerned, is to challenge him with proof that he's awake.

Once, a long time after this, I saw Bobby driving in a car with a new boyfriend. When they got closer I could see they were both naked. Jack and Bobby were driving down a crowded street in the middle of summer—a street from a dream. Dream Street.

Jack stopped the car and Bobby climbed out through the window and sat on the hood for a minute, for a reaction. Then he climbed back in. It was too funny and out of context to be sexy. But then it was sexy, too, because it was him, and this was the way Bobby liked to present himself to the world.

Before that car and that boyfriend, Bobby sashayed down a dirt road every Monday night, away from AA and all its principles toward me where I lived on Atkins Lane. There was a skylight that was flush with the edge of the sea, and I could smell the sea on my sheets. And the sun was there, too, mixed up in the smell of the sea.

Bobby talked about his acting career gone bust in New York City. He went to graduate school and joined a theater company. Then Bobby met an actor/addict whom he loved. Then he drank. Bobby came to Provincetown to find sobriety. He didn't know that the sea wouldn't give him sobriety automatically, but we both knew there are days when the sea can seem like being sober—calm, with the old terror underneath—like any mirror.

The Last Two People on Earth:
An Apocalyptic Vaudeville

(Abrons Arts Center, New York, 2013)

We went to see *The Last Two People on Earth: An Apocalyptic Vaudeville* the other night. It was playing at the Abrons Arts Center at the very end of Grand Street and appeared like a mirage on an airfield.

The last two people on earth are Mandy Patinkin and Taylor Mac. They are a vaudeville act.

What else could the last two people on earth be but a vaudeville act?

My grandfather was in vaudeville. He made the song "When the Red, Red Robin (Comes Bob, Bob, Bobbin' Along)" famous. It was the first song my mother taught me, and I sang it on command whenever she missed her father, which, most of the time, was when she was driving. Badly. Something about the past made memory happen for my mother in a car.

In *The Last Two People on Earth*, Messrs. Patinkin and Taylor sing other people's songs and opt for singing more than talking—which is a way of saying that conversation ended with the world.

The songs are about what they remembered about being alive: joyfully/woefully. And it was political theater, too—critical of America. It reminded me of Brecht. It was good to see that political thinking—real political thinking, engaging with ideas and resistance—had survived the flood of the play. The men grew to love each other through this series of songs, which is why they didn't have to say anything. Love is an action, they seemed to be saying, like singing.

The songs in the vaudeville act were written by people like Randy Newman, Peter Allen, Rogers and Hammerstein, Paul Simon, R.E.M., and Stephen Sondheim. There was a beautiful song by Patty Griffin called "Making Pies."

The Last Two People on Earth was one of those works of art that performed the wondrous act of folding some great sadness into happiness, which felt like—after hearing every song—the best way of making certain we would remember it.

Here were the last songs anybody would ever sing. And as Mandy and Taylor paddled away in their inflatable raft, aimed at the heartbroken vaudeville horizon, their last song was "Row, Row, Row Your Boat," which we all know ends with the truest line ever written about life on Earth: it's but a dream.

Horses Between Hangovers

I came from New York to the racetracks of Florida as a groom, but also as a poet, one who wasn't writing very much. I wrote mostly in my head back then (this was the late '70s) and listened to the Southern weather come down hard through the trees at Hialeah Park in Miami that first winter out of New York. I lived in my Vista Cruiser before hooking up with an outfit that could give me a room and—if I was lucky—a horse to take care of that could run. It took some time to end up in a good stable. And I was young, and the timing of youth has a dream-like rhythm to it. Anything can happen.

Or so it seemed the day I got a job working for Woody Stephens, who had one of the best training outfits in America. And though his was a good barn envied by anyone who worked the backstretch, there was never a sense of hierarchy on the racetrack. The grooms and exercise riders, and even sometimes assistant trainers, would pull the same broken-down folding chairs into the shed rows under the palms each night and pass around stories about a horse that was a rising star, or a horse that had fallen from grace, or a trainer who had said to a drug-addled groom, "You must be drinking your bathwater." Then there was the famously rank colt, D'Accord, who had—so this particular story went—picked up a hot walker by the scruff of his neck, dragged him to the back of the stall, and stomped him to death.

All writing starts in the body before it emerges as language. And for me, it started with those warm winter nights at Hialeah, when I would listen to stories fall from the mouths of black and white grooms who lived between happiness and the next van ride with their horses to Calder or Gulf Stream, where the easier races were run. Dreaming was easier then. And we were all—all of us—dreamers.

We dreamed awake.

Which made it so there was always something unreal about the work. The morning light trembling in the trees would float over the straw of freshly bedded stalls, and you moved slowly around horses in the morning.

And later—in what feels like a folding over of time—it's suddenly afternoon and the day feels more formal because you are watching those same horses from their morning run form part of that day's racing card.

I was writing poems in my head about what it was like to have nothing in front of me but horses, about how I had to move my body through a stall in a way so a horse wouldn't hurt me—how that became a metaphor for times in my life when I needed to tell myself: *take care.* But I didn't write any of those ideas down—I was too drunk a lot of time, barely vertical. Life was horses between hangovers.

At the track, I had no paper, no pen, and certainly no computer. Florida bombarded me with heat and routine that got mixed into a body on its way to being broken. I just kept moving forward until I left the racetrack, finally, and stopped drinking, finally.

Then with horses gone, they entered my sleeping life—in dreams—which is where I found the first sentence that would lead to all the other sentences of what would later become a book: *I ran away.*

Somebody called me after reading *Track Conditions* and wanted to tell me that he'd been on the track, too—gyp tracks, mostly—as I had been in the beginning. This man wanted to know the real names of people in the book. Some of them—the daredevils, the ones who got me to change. But most of all, he wanted to know whatever happened to Richard, my racetrack lover—the guy who got me hitched to a star that could only right and relight itself in the winner's circle.

So we talked a little about track life. And eventually I felt sort of put upon because (and here was the reason for the call, which is always the reason for the call) he'd written a book about the racetrack, too. And he's not really a writer, etc., etc. And before he could officially ask, I said, "Of course I'll read it. And if I like it, I'll finish it," the whole time while talking to him looking through my mind for the room with the cot and the radio at the end of the barn where I used to crash after a day of horses and drinking.

Finally, I told him I appreciated the call. I heard in his what must-have-been-75-year-old Tallahassee drawl the soul of someone who was once in love with the sport of kings, and how that life that wasn't for him anymore. He was my brother, there in that long-ago life, so inadequately lit no matter what racetrack you worked on, or what bar they just kicked you out of because last call had been called, called and called. He was my brother back from the races calling to tell me he stayed alive, too.

Handsome

Richard Coatney, Ocala, FL, 1978

Richard and I lived in a trailer called The First Lady that sat on Ruthie's farm in Ocala, Florida when we were breaking yearlings at a training center down the road. We got to Ocala by way of trainers Mutt and Ruby Raidy who would later take the horses to Latonia racetrack in Kentucky and River Downs across the Ohio River in Cincinnati—a track where, Richard used to joke, the horses were on everything but roller skates to get them over the finish line.

I've always loved this picture of Richard—in his boozy, smokey element and the sneakers I bought him that Christmas because he didn't own a pair of what I considered in my idiosyncratic take to be cool shoes. He looks handsome in the Polaroid—the most handsome, I think, I'd ever known him, which in 1978 had only been a year and change.

I've written about Richard here and there—notes for something—about his shocking death last April, when a car crashed into a van taking him to the airport in Dayton, Ohio. According to news reports, he was killed instantly. And since then, I've been looking furiously for this picture which I put somewhere I'd never remember because I had no real reason to look at it again. But key to death's nostalgia is how it always ushers in letters and photographs and so, I finally was able to get my hands on the picture today.

It's such an old picture which makes it sad, of course. And the quality of scratch marks makes it wistful in a way that almost clouds the way I can see it—knowing that he isn't anymore. And another sad, because after 11 years of being partners in chaos and witnesses to some occasional and astonishing beauty, it's the only picture I've ever had of him. We never thought about taking pictures. The first rule of drinking is to forget and the first rule of photography is to remember.

Part of what I think makes Richard handsome in the picture—after the red hair that offsets the blue eyes—is the beard which, in all the years I was with him, he trimmed now and then but never shaved off completely. What story was his face telling that his beard wouldn't let anyone listen to? He looked like a man with a beard, but he also looked like someone I would never see—a secret truth that neither of us even thought about discussing.

Until, as it happened, a few years after we broke up I went to visit him where he was living in Pelion, SC, and he greeted me at the airport with the face I was never allowed to see before. And I realized immediately that the beard was his way of completing a chin—looking at it now—that didn't seem quite finished—the same way I had to warn the barber to always leave my hair long enough to cover the rabbit-shaped bald spot on the right side of my head.

We surprised each other in that way when you looked around, other people were always surprising each other in an airport: in greetings, in departures. And looking at him with a younger face, and him looking at me, and the weight I'd gained, was like saying hello to our somewhat revised doppelgangers. We were the same people to ourselves, but completely different people to each other. I had become more serious about writing and he had become someone who was taking photographs and teaching painting to children.

And in the car, driving to his slightly haunted-looking bungalow in the woods, I realized that we had come to the official beginning of being happy without each other. The break-up allowed us to get back to what we yearned for but held off reaching far enough to grab it because the next drink was always closer and now we had both been at least a few years sober.

We had, in the airport moment, become two people in the fullest expressions of not being able to hide from each other anymore.

Airports and Funerals in Sobriety

One winter morning 100 years ago, waiting for a flight to Seattle, I realized there's something about sunlight falling into the long hallway of an airport that always reminds me of early sobriety. I don't know why that is, particularly, since in the beginning I went to meetings only at night and in the dark. Kirk and I would go to a midnight meeting in Times Square and then across the street to the Howard Johnson's that was—until they ripped it down a few years ago—an historical landmark of my very non-historical youth. We went to the meeting after the meeting, as we used to call it, over coffee and what the management touted as the best lemon meringue pie in New York. There was a realization in those early days of not drinking anymore that we were going to miss something if we went home to sleep. At the Howard Johnson's we were using that energy to keep an idea in flight, rather than wondering where we were going to get the money to get really drunk.

I have never taken my sobriety for granted, but sometimes I forget what it actually costs. I've been sober for a long time and have seen a lot of sunlight pouring through many airports and over fields of grass and the occasional summertime body of water. My happiness is different now and comes in a different strength than that manic happiness that jagged hari-kari-ingly with vodka or beer. I still don't believe I could have just one drink, so I haven't even tried in almost 40 years. So this morning I am grateful for the water and the coffee and these suede boots that—now that I think on it—have never taken a single drunken step.

A few years later, there was another great day to be sober. It started with a drive on the Taconic Parkway to a funeral in Hopewell Junction, New York. My brother-in-law's mother had died and Andrew and I drove up to support him and his family. The trees on the Taconic looked miraculous, every branch covered in just enough ice to make it seem we were driving through a glass menagerie of something—which, just then, looked like trees.

After the funeral mass, we got flowers to put on the casket before it descended into the ground. I was holding a white chrysanthemum and Andrew was holding a yellow rose and when there were no flowers left among the living we walked away. My brother-in-law stood there alone in the cold sunlight and Andrew and I walked to the car and joined a line of cars driving to the reception—that awkward ceremony of friends and strangers all joined together in a chorus of memories about the recently departed.

One of the shining lights of sobriety has been my ability to feel living in all its beauty, sadness, and complexity; to stand with a white chrysanthemum and look up at an avenue of trees made out of ice and to love the world of what is here and what departs the world; to experience sadness without reaching for a solution to sadness; to join myself to the sadness.

And, if the funeral or the grandeur of the natural world weren't enough to make me grateful, going to the movies that same night to see *Rachel Getting Married* certainly brought gratitude close. The film brings to life the terror and narcissism of addiction with a hand-held camera and a script written—the way *Days of Wine and Roses* was written—from inside of a disease—imbued with the sense that surviving this world isn't only a personal achievement, but an artistic one, too.

Ruby

My dog—our dog—Ruby is dying. She just got up from one of her many naps—the only time her breathing doesn't sound so labored—and I think, oh good, she's awake, she's not dying, when of course I know that she's awake and is of course still dying. Her shortness of breath is back, and we will find out through the indecency of an X-ray taken the next day that Ruby is drowning from a tidal wave filling her lungs—congestive heart failure. And the vet recommends we let her go.

Today. Today?

Ruby's dying brought about an abrupt end not only to her wonderful, Zen-like self (she would stand in the middle of a room and just gaze, sometimes for 20 minutes), but also to the end of a specific window of time for both of us in one life, braided in play and more than occasional awe and tenderness. And maybe it's too sentimental to put it that way—sentimental even to be writing about the death of a dog because its universal patent on sadness is such a cliche—but none of it feels sentimental to me. Sadness always dares us to be sentimental, but the beginning of grief is too hopped up on reality, with no trace of the nostalgia that happens later when sadness, in review, is only the early aspect of hard fact.

And the hard fact is something that my friend, Chase, told me after Ruby died—that having a dog is a tragedy waiting to happen. We love our animals more than we can ever love the world and Ruby's death has jarred me into the oddness of a newness to time—how each hour now—until it isn't—is just like this—the hour before it. And there's a field of silence, which isn't about the absence of the chirping sound she made whenever she drank water, but about the absence of *presence*.

When she was dying, one of my sadnesses was watching Ruby try to get comfortable enough so that she could get her back end in a resting position and then put her head on my ankle, just as she was dozing off. I've been in bed with my dog, dozing on and off for three years, which meant that I brought everything I needed each day to bed with me— every book, every essay I was writing, all the editing I've been doing on two books of true crime, the Zoom meetings, the phone calls—all of it—like this, together, in our bed in Newport, RI, with my noble beast.

I had some inner sense when we first got to Newport—due in no small part to my own sudden sense of mortality as I approach the last act—that Ruby was going to die soon. She was already 12 years old, and French bulldogs don't last much longer than that. Every French bulldog owner I met on the street when we lived in New York would warn me about that, the number 12, until, after this year, when Ruby turned 13, I fantastically thought that maybe she'd/we'd escaped her death. If she could make it 13, she'd make it to 14, easy. And then on to forever. Gone is the opposite of forever, but it's too short a word to hold all that it means, which is *disappeared*. On Friday, Ruby disappeared.

I asked my friend, Fr. Spencer Reece, poet and Vicar of Wickford, RI, do dogs know they're going to die? Is this the key to the locked box of mystery of why we love them so much, and to such overwhelming distraction? Because in the end, it's that fact of their not knowing about death that puts our own dying on hold—in dog years, anyway. And with Ruby gone, I've been thrown back into my own dying—which comes to me as a winding down, which means moments of thinking more about what *happened to* me already than *what's going to happen*—looking at photographs, reading letters. Going back to see what I've brought with me from the past into today.

One thing I do know, because it had happened already, is that my dog disappearing has freed me—at least in a utilitarian sense. I can't bring anything to bed anymore because she's not there to need me. And I have an office that I haven't been using that I will now be using for writing, and a living room for watching movies instead of watching everything in bed. And there's a lightness to the freedom of what it's like to move through unstructured time. But I find myself having to rush through domesticity—like folding the laundry or cleaning the dishes or emptying the litter box or moving the boxes of too many books down to the basement. Rushing, because I don't want to stop long enough to think of Ruby and begin again the coming-out-of-nowhere weeping.

I'm dehydrated from weeping, rewired from weeping, illogical from weeping. I want to intellectualize grief to not have to feel its waves crashing into me every time I side-look at the picture of her on the fridge and her favorite throw pillow with the lobster needlepoint.

My husband's favorite photograph has always been that of Ruby lying on top of me the day she came home with us on MLK's birthday in 2011. And from that photograph on, and at some point, every morning, I would hold my puppy on top of me through all of the names I ever had for her—but mostly settling on her truest name: Monkey. I held on to her just long enough to feel her weight become part of my weight, part of me, my best self.

And so, it was

And so, it is

And so it shall be.

There's no such thing as a wrong note, as long as you're singing.

    --Pete Seeger

Movie Rain and Movie Snow

1.

Henry James famously said that the two most beautiful words in English are summer afternoon. Let rain come next. It's been raining for two days in New York and I don't know what it is about rain in New York, but it is always nostalgic. Whenever this happens, whenever it rains, I see New York through the filter of wet weather as a place I knew best in my youth. Through water I can see the buildings that are still there on 8th Street, on Lexington Avenue, in a way that I never think about when the glare of the sun points them out. Rain is the weather of memory and of self-reflection.

Vincent Van Gogh has a painting called "Rain." I'll never forget the first time I saw it at the Metropolitan Museum of Art. It's a huge painting—probably the largest canvas Van Gogh ever put paint on, and it's aspect—the way Van Gogh has painted the rain—is as ethereal as it is physical. Those stabs of shortened light look as though they are trying to obscure the land as much as they are trying to bring it into focus, because that's where all the motion is. Van Gogh made a still-life that backs up against the thing it has to absorb to be seen.

But back in New York, where I live outside of Van Gogh, rain doesn't look like this. It looks, most of the time, like the rain from the last scene in *Breakfast at Tiffany's* where Audrey Hepburn is looking through a torrential pouring of the stuff for the cat named Cat she just threw away.

2.

Of course, I can never feel objective about snow after seeing "Citizen Kane"—which, somewhere near the end (or is it the beginning—the whole film feels kaleidoscopic in the mind)—presents a scene of snow for its explanation of a sled named Rosebud, still vibratory in meaning: tyrants had childhoods.

Four Versions of Night in a Movie

Some movies get the night better than life does. Other things that movies get better are betrayal, crime, and slapstick. And sex, probably, except for theoretical sex, which life gets better.

I am thinking of the movie night we enter for the dazzling and famous opening shot—in one take—in *Touch of Evil* and Janet Leigh and the white of the Mexican street leading to the American border that counterpoints the falling of the night on the car's trunk that's holding the bomb, which is the only other character at the start of *Touch of Evil*.

Or I'm thinking of the claustrophobic night inside the cottage from *The Miracle Worker* where Annie Sullivan has taken Helen Keller to bring her into the more combustible world by removing her from the other more broken world where her family broods like a family in an O'Neill play, in black and white—a night that swings from rambunctiousness to lullaby: *Mama's gonna buy you a mockingbird.*

Or I am thinking of the brother and sister, John and Pearl, from *Night of the Hunter*, who finally set themselves free from the tyrannical false God played by Robert Mitchum, as they drift on a river in a rowboat making its way to an awaiting Lillian Gish in a night of stars that look as if they're reflected by the water onto the sky and not the other way around. And Pearl is singing something she might be making up called "Pretty Fly," whose otherworldly beauty sounds like a song from the future.

And I am thinking of the last night, the best night in my pantheon of movie nights. Giulietta Masina is walking through a dream of trees and music in *Nights of Cabiria* with every known expression for the human face exalting her into a surprising *buona sera* from a stranger—and exalted again—led through a winding dream to a threshold of a most specific longing. And the light that is always anonymous—for that is what the night brings, every anonymity, like stray cats that know how the story got written. And the dark that turns anyone into the sleepwalker who has stayed awake by looking hard into the everlasting.

David Jones

There was this beautiful sunset in Wellfleet Harbor in the '90s that I can't have anymore.

I was doing a one-man show called *10,000 Hands Have Touched Me* that nobody liked (cold, cannibalized from older work).

My friend, who I was in love with, used to swim with me before I had to get on stage and attempt to make my life sound like hunger or beauty or noise.

My friend and I swam out to where it was hard to distinguish the water from the sky, out to that part of living where you stop talking.

I would rock him in my arms until he became the lightest human being in the world.

Years later, he washed up on the rocks at the breakwater end of Provincetown. He was murdered, some people said. Or, he'd ODed.

When he was the lightest human being in the world, I loved him and knew I would never tell him that I loved him, which made love fade and come back like the lighthouse beam that trembles on a wave.

When he was the lightest human being in the world, he was David at the moment of the idea of David, before something or somebody dropped his body at the end of the street where the water started.

Newported

After my parents divorced when I was around 10, my mother lived in New York, and my father bought a house in Branford, Connecticut on the Long Island Sound, which must have been the first time I fell in love with the sea. That I could see the Sound across the street from the house meant swimming and sand and dreaming awake in that other world of the sun beating down and me and the gang of other kids I ran around with some of those days. And in its mysterious way, having a landscape like that to live inside made it incapable for me to think of living anywhere else—except that I did, when I visited my mother in New York two or three weekends a month.

     I had to wait another 50 years to see the sea again—in Provincetown, living on a writing fellowship. Then, after the fellowship ended, I moved back to New York for a teaching job and it would be another ten years before I could see the Cape again, living in a one-room cottage that my husband and I were able to buy, sitting at the edge of the bay where the air smelled of beach roses during the day and the smoke of bonfires lighting up the strip of shore at night, connecting the end of Provincetown to the beginning of Truro. A lot of my primal longing feels palpable when it gets tied up with the sea, missing the sea. Still, I wonder if it could be considered longing when it wells up in the present—facing the ocean right now, sentient and insignificant and in one piece.

     Most of my life has been spent in New York. But when the opportunity came up, in May of 2020, to move to Newport, RI, we decided to go for it and leave the city. This meant we had to put the apartment we loved on the market at the height of a pandemic when people were fleeing New York, certainly not a buyer's market. We moved because Andrew was offered a job managing an upscale restaurant, but we still had to pay the mortgage until the apartment sold and that took more than a year and overlapped with us living in Newport, where we had to pay rent.

     Before we moved here, the few friends we had in the building back in the city were sure it had to do with the virus. But really, Covid had nothing to do with it. And besides, I'm most definitely a go-down-with-the-ship kind of guy. The quarantine didn't cast any isolated pall—just the opposite. We'd become punch-drunk recluses who loved staying indoors, watching movies, reading, writing, making meals at home, and experiencing a languid and metaphysical dismantling of time. How does one enter a field like that—a cosmic field of scrambled time? Time was elastic to the point that we, like many people, weren't sure what day it was. By all accounts, we were all living in what the duo, Seals and Croft once titled an album, the year of Sunday.

We'd been to Newport before—one impulsive frigid weekend years ago, off-season, when the town was wet and gray. We stayed at Gurney's, a luxury destination spot, I'd guessed, seeing at it was connected to town via a bridge across the harbor that led to the mysteriously named Goat Island. And we took in the town's famous Cliff Walk—a 3.5 mile hike along the ocean on one side and mansions from the Gilded Age on the other. Those mansions for the rich and the dead were even more dramatic that day—painted against the storm-gray sky and looking haunted, whether they had already been deemed haunted or not.

Tourists love to traipse through the "cottages," as they are preposterously called, and walk from one room into the next with the practiced solemnity of mourners lined up to view the decorated statesman lying in state. I know how much people enjoy a sunny walk through an empty mansion, but for me, every room looked about as comfortable to live in as a straitjacket. There's an overwhelming sense I often have of being too alive for anything like the cloying stillness of a room where nothing has changed for more than a century, too alive to sleep in the bed in the room or sit at the desk to write a letter or to pull back the curtains to look at the ocean—curtains as heavy as those Edward Hopper painted in "First Row Orchestra," and "New York Movie."

The furnishings in these bedrooms look either fossilized or like something that could kill you slowly. A hairbrush doesn't look clean, or there's a piece of its handle broken off in such a way that animates it, so it could be used as a shiv; the throne of a simple chair that will try to eat you alive, absorbing you in its sucking, brittle velvet. And if you're standing at the door, not going in, restless now from having seen enough, the rooms look as if they've been ironed and spray-starched into the irreversible seriousness of a still-life.

An empty mansion today feels more like a tomb honoring the architectural ideal of its famous era, The Gilded Age—which is as much about the materialism of the rich as it is about the disturbing social ills of poverty and political corruption that were just a scratch beneath the gold gilding.

I do love houses, though—even big houses—and there is an extraordinary array of houses all over Newport and the rest of Aquidneck Island, in Middletown and Portsmouth. The house that Andrew and I found had a great apartment, and we took it right away, based only on the pictures we saw online. It's on the first floor of a small Victorian, flooded with light, mainly in the room I write in, which is the first and only room I've ever had to write in. Every writer I know has their own devoted space, and now I see why it's so important.

This is the place where the surrounding makes up what you know best—the things that matter to you—books, paper, photographs—and in addition, for me, a framed letter from William Maxwell after I wrote to him asking if he would read the memoir I had written about life on the racetrack. Maxwell's letter contains this sentence—which feels, whenever I read it, like a breaking open of a place where a great truth has been lying in wait: "But once, when I was in my early twenties, I had the experience of riding on a lovely horse, a mare named Diana, in a stable in a suburb of Chicago. I lost my heart to her and—because this is a true love story—never saw her again."

To get a better lay of the land and to see the rest of Aquidneck Island, of which Newport is one of three places—Middletown and Portsmouth the other two—I got a job delivering pizzas that took me everywhere and gave me what racetrackers fondly refer to as "walking around money"—which is only just a little more than chump change.

Here's what I discovered about Newport and Middletown during my short-lived pizza gig:

1. Almost all the houses have doorbells that look like they
    wouldn't work and actually don't—hanging off the house or
    in a disarray of shattered plastic, cracked enough to let the
    circuitry through.

2. Almost all the houses are unnumbered—as though the towns were small enough for everybody to know who lived in which houses without needing an address.
3. Almost all the streets—except for Thames and Bellevue and Spring—run in both directions, which is confusing as to how and why—as those streets are almost too narrow to hold even one-way traffic. The few streets that are one-way amazingly permit parking, but only if you can get half the car to sit up on the curb.

There's more to find out about the place where I live—especially about the house I stumbled upon the other day on my almost daily ride along the spectacular Ocean Drive, where I looked for a place to meditate for 20 minutes. It was a shell of a house, really; maybe the owners ran out of money to finish the renovation. The house had what felt like a private view of the ocean and I found, amazingly, an open door and went inside and turned my phone's video on to capture the vastness of the space, consisting of gravel floors, fireplaces, cathedral heights, and gorgeous beams. It made me think, again, of William Maxwell, who, in his glorious novel, "So Long, See You Tomorrow," talks about walking through an unfinished house from his childhood:

> "And I had the agreeable feeling, as I went from one room to the next by walking through the wall instead of a doorway, or looked up and saw blue sky through the rafters, that I had found a way to get around the way things were."

Living in Newport includes having a deck that oversees birds and squirrels, a profusion of daily rabbits, and the occasional opossum. I've never had so many daily encounters with house finches, tufted titmice, sparrows, and the more than occasional cardinal that come to the feeders we hung like lanterns around the backyard. The first couple of weeks after moving in, two or three birds, on as many occasions, suddenly swooped through the mouth of the wood-burning stove and into the living room. One bird—a sparrow—stayed frozen on a windowsill long enough for me to take it in my hand, go with it outside, and sit with it for

15 minutes until its heart relaxed and it suddenly flew out of my hand—back into its soaring life. But then, as if to confuse the memory, two days later, a house finch hit the glass door to the deck so hard that it died.

Of course, the two summers I've had so far here have been glorious, and the winters have been short, without biting too badly. And, when birds aren't arriving via the wood stove, it's a great luxury to have a fire whenever we've needed a fire.

Andrew lit the first one while I was in another room and then came to me and told me to close my eyes. Then, ceremonially, he took me by the hand and led us to the part of the house I could feel getting gradually warmer. The tenderness of the ceremony matched the sight of our two cats and French bulldog sprawled across the floor, hypnotized by another light besides the sun falling on them.

"Do you want a fire?" I asked Andrew, on one of the coldest nights we've had here. "Sure," he said, though he still had to be the one to get it going in his butch way I never can never manage to duplicate. The stove and its blazing probably gave us a closer feeling of the strange intimacy that came with pandemic life—a way of seeing the people we live with, if we live with any, that seems more solid and necessary.

And somehow I've gotten to be the age where people start living in retirement country—if only experiencing it as a state of mind. For me, it means that Newport is the place where, after living all those years in Provincetown and New York, and the fact that I'm one year past at the doorway of 70 years old, will be where I'll die. Until then, I can pick up with the sea at the place where we left off.

William Maxwell

My favorite writer is William Maxwell and in 1997 I wanted to send him a copy of a book I wrote because he'd made me so happy as a reader and, since this was my first book of prose, I felt that his writing had influenced mine—if only a little.

He did read my book. And then my favorite writer wrote me a letter, which I framed, suffering over which frame to choose, one that would honor my new favorite possession. And I decided that everything around the type should be white so that the crossed-out words would stand out since—its greatest charm—it had been composed on a typewriter.

The letter hangs over my writing desk, which is really not a writing desk because both Andrew and I use it for whatever we need a desk for. I have never had a writing desk my entire writing life. I have also never gone to a writers colony, or had lunches delivered to me in a picnic basket by birds who have magically set it down at my front door.

Here's the letter:

8/8/1997

Dear Mr. Klein:

    I enjoyed your memoir very much indeed. I suppose
it is too sentimental to be plausible, but I couldn't help
feeling that the death of Swale was in some way related
to your removal. I had no idea that ~~race horses~~ were so
fragile.

    Because I was not an experienced rider, on the infrequent
occasions that I have gone horseback riding, I have usually
ended up with a nag ~~that~~ insisted on eating grass when he
should have been trotting, and had a tendency to bite the
other horses. But once, when I was in my early twenties,
I had the experience of riding on a lovely horse, a mare
named Diana, in a stable in a suburb of Chicago. I lost
my heart to her and---because this is a true love story---
never saw her again.

    During my childhood, the man who lived next door was
a veterinarian. He also bought and sold horses to the army
during the First World War. I went to the races with him
in Chicago once, and after I had no more money to bet, I
had a hunch on a horse called Building Trades. I had hot
and cold flashes. The horse paid twenty to one.

                My best to you,

                William Maxwell

What I love about the letter is how it stays clear of whatever
William Maxwell might have thought of my writing apart from saying
that he enjoyed the book. Instead, he conjures up his own horse story as
a way of saying *hello, I can see you.* That yes—he sees horses, too.

Racetracks in America

When I was writing *Track Conditions*, a memoir about my mostly drunken experiences while employed as a groom to Swale, the 1984 Kentucky Derby winner, a strange thing happened to my body—it returned to the way it looked during the period the book was written about. Through diet and exercise (two practices foreign to me most of my life), I lost 40 pounds. It was as if the occasion of writing about that crucial time—the hinge between inebriation and sobriety—caused my body and mind to physically let go of its story. Or was it that, by writing *that* chapter of my life, I could once again inhabit the body that survived it?

All memoirs are about hunger—a hunger not just to *know*, but to let some things come closer—to comprehend the narrative of a life that, more often than not, reads only as fragments. As a writer, I was looking for a golden thread, though also an epiphany that would explain or resolve the gravitational pull of my life, and state of mind, during the seven-year period I worked on racetracks in America. What happened then was harrowing, both the actual events and what those events echoed from an even more awful time before the horses: an abusive stepfather, my mother's death, and a romantic partner who couldn't stay—the last and most hurtful strike against my consciousness and sense of well-being. The racetrack was the perfect metaphor for the wilderness of my own mind.

But the track was also my last stand, the last place I had my last drink. And I knew that by returning there in writing I would find the answer to the question of why, at that intersection of living and dying, I finally decided to stop being the person who was killing me. I would also say that writing prose helped answer a question that poetry—all I'd written up to that point, anyway—couldn't answer.

Apart from my weight falling away, the other great and surprising change that came with the memoir was discipline—for a while anyway. I had to inhabit a linear world every day—something I had never done before as a writer. My poems generally come whenever they feel like it—when my life can't resist writing them down. But that deep well—wherever the poems come from—takes its own time to fill up before I can draw from it.

Memoirs are the natural place for a poet to begin prose. Look at them all: *The Liar's Club* and *Lit* by Mary Karr, *The Guardians* by Sarah Manguso, and *I Wore the Ocean in the Shape of a Girl* by Kelle Groom— all terrific books and all written by writers whose first time out of the gate was a book of poems. And not just poets; for many novelists, too, that first book of prose is a memoir—disguised though it may be. The impulse to present *MY LIFE* in narrative is the trigger for a lot of writers.

When I finished *Wild*, Cheryl Strayed's best-selling memoir about how she faced the death of her mother, my friend Sallie, who lives in Plymouth, asked if I'd read Cheryl's novel, *Torch*. I told her I hadn't, and probably wouldn't, because of the bad habit I have (bias, whatever) of not reading fiction written by writers of a great book of non-fiction (note that I don't say *creative non-fiction* because I think, as a phrase, it's redundant and precious).

I don't read such novels because the memoirs almost always turn out to be that writer's best work. And it isn't just the popularity of the genre that attracts me either, or the movement of the prose, or the lucidity of the subject matter, or the beauty of its syntax, turning a sentence inside out, or any of that. Though, of course, all of that does make non-fiction better. It's the simple fact that when I'm reading the other stuff—the fiction—I know something that the person who wrote it knows, too: it's all a lie.

Edouard Leve

I'm a poet who likes paragraphs.

What I like about the paragraph is that it's so unlike me. It's a picture of a kind of order, and it looks like a safe place to land—a well-made raft in the middle of a lake called thinking. But how do I get back to shore?

The block of thinking that a paragraph represents is longer than any of the longest lines of poetry because it's an island brought about through an outbreak of sentences. So there's a logic to the paragraph, and it can be one sentence long or many sentences long.

The length of the sentence is also an island and depends on the way the end of it sounds to the person who wrote it—as it is with all islands one chooses to land on. You stay for a while. You get off. You come back.

I'm sure there are rules to writing a paragraph, but I have—if I ever even knew—forgotten what they are and why they're important. I have also forgotten the rules for writing an essay because I started writing essays before I read somewhere that there was a way, or some ways, of writing an essay. Something formulaic.

There are rules—only rules, it seems—for writing screenplays—more rules than for the essay or the poem or the novel, even, which is why people get more money for writing screenplays than they do for writing essays or things that are not screenplays. I can't imagine writing a screenplay, although it would be nice to make money for writing something someday. I can't figure out if it is day or night or day for night or why the hero has to be knocked around in order for the life they're building before our eyes to make any sense. So, I've stayed with poems, and sometimes I write paragraphs.

I've been thinking about the paragraph a lot lately because I can't get one out of my head. I just finished the astonishing memoir, *Autoportrait* by Edouard Leve (translated from the French by Lorin Stein), which is a book-length paragraph. Here is the beginning of it:

"When I was young, I thought *Life: A User's Manual* would teach me how to live and *Suicide: A User's Manual* how to die. I have spent three years and three months abroad. I prefer to look to my left. I have a friend who gets off on betrayal. The end of a trip leaves me with a sad aftertaste, the same as the end of a novel. I forget things I don't like. I may have spoken, without even knowing it, to someone who killed someone. I look down dead-end streets. I am not afraid of what comes at the end of life. I don't really listen to what people are saying. I am surprised when someone gives me a nickname, and we hardly know each other. I am slow to notice when someone mistreats me; it's always so surprising. Evil is somehow unreal. I archive. I spoke to Salvador Dali when I was two. Competition does not drive me. To describe my life precisely would take longer than to live it."

Besides being a 117-page paragraph (very short for a book, very long for paragraph, and one of its major delights), *Autoportrait* has the urgency of someone who knows they are going to die soon. Anatole Broyard based his book, *Intoxicated By My Illness,* on that knowing, and Harold Brodkey faced dying with *This Wild Darkness: The Story of My Death*, a book that emerged out of the last days of his life with AIDS. And more famously, Sylvia Plath wrote *Ariel*.

What Leve has done—more than any book I have ever read—is pare down living to its most essential unit of measure: declaration—a sentence following another sentence declaring the love for something—all of which would come an abrupt halt in the two weeks after Leve's second book, *Suicide*, a novel, was handed to the publisher when the writer took his own life.

Leve's book is a fever dream brought on by sentences that are so haunting, or brief, and utterly surprising. The book follows no decipherable logic and concerns the author's childhood, people he knew and/or loved, somebody who got lost, some travels, his hunger and openness around sex, ideas for projects (he was known primarily as a photographer), definitions for loneliness and fulfillment, etc., etc. In other words, it's a book about the metronomic habit of culmination. There is no story to such a book, only an invitation to stay in its thrall.

On the face of it, *Autoportrait* sounds completely arbitrary, self-indulgent, and a waste of time, which is always the verdict I receive when I make the mistake of giving a brief description of the book to students before I assign it. But the book is anything but a waste of time because you have to teach yourself how to read it, which is similar to how it feels to go through a day, hitting all its intermittencies, be they logical or not. Some would find writing that mirrors such things journalistic or soul-rattling, but I found it audacious and weirdly refreshing.

I first read an excerpt from *Autoportrait* in an issue of *The Paris Review*, and it was immediately clear what Leve was up to—a grammarian's trick with a black and white scarf of typed sentences fluttering out to a horizon of collected statements. But what wasn't clear was how any particular excerpt—the way it happens with most excerpts—could give you a sense of the whole book. Almost any excerpt from *Autoportrait* does, in fact, give you a sense of the whole book because you could open it to any page and just start reading. It's a book that was written in more than one direction.

In some ways, *Autoportrait* is a variation on Joe Brainard's famous anti-memoir, *I Remember,* which, if you don't know it, is made up entirely of sentences that start with the words "I remember." Leve's is not as tender a book as Brainard's, and *I Remember* has become so commonly used as a place to start with a group writing exercise, that I have begun reaching for something else because I can't read or talk about it anymore.

I don't want to remember *I Remember* because I remember how much I loved it when it first hit me.

It's a Brigadoon affair, really, and after your own pleasure for a text, the second pleasure arrives when you've watched somebody else discover the book.

Leve's paragraph—his book, like Brainard's—is also a collection: a list of facts from living memory. And its beauty happens in the after imagery of read sentences, which stand there naked because of how impossible it would be to change anything in its syntax. These are sentences with the feeling of having just stopped moving. And because the writing is so bald, and the string of declaratives so closely follows a subconscious more than the revisionary mind, one that has come to its final version, *Autoportrait* is—while not strictly in a literary sense—still a poetic act.

Somebody once asked Gary Snyder during an Academy of American Poets Poetry Forum in New York what the difference was between poetry and prose—a question I pray stops being asked—and Snyder said, "You can force prose." If poetry is something you can't force and prose is something you can, Leve, with *Autoportrait*, nevertheless does both—forcing something that triggers something else that just can't be stopped.

How do you know you aren't improvising?

　　—*Steve Paxton*

Nick Flynn

I went to a screening of *Being Flynn* in Chicago years ago and had that exhilarating and yet eerie experience of seeing somebody I knew in real life presented as a character in a movie. How strange it was to watch scenes that were built from actual conversations I had with somebody I knew named Nick Flynn in Provincetown.

It was a hard movie to watch, even if I was already familiar with the material. The film is based on Nick's bestselling memoir, *Another Bullshit Night in Suck City*, an account of his relationship with his homeless father, who was living off and on at Pine Street Inn, the men's shelter in Boston where Nick himself used to work (the movie changed the locale to New York).

When I met Nick more than 20 years ago during a potluck dinner at the Fine Arts Work Center in Provincetown, I thought that he, too, was homeless—wild and unmoored, trying to get clean and sober, and just then embarking on a serious commitment to writing poetry. He was working on a boat that was dry docked at the end of Bradford Street but would hopefully, soon, hit the water again. I'm pretty sure Nick was living on it, but he may have found somewhere more sheltered at night.

Over the years, Nick and I became good friends and he's remained remarkably the same person even as the frenzy of fame and fortune rushed in to meet him—a very different life. And as it is for so many of us who banded together, his is a resolutely saved life. I kept being hit with the realization of that hard knowledge, his saved life, as I was watching *Being Flynn,* and struck harder still by the knowledge that both he and his father live now and then at different ends of the same boat.

I ran into Nick the morning after the movie in the hotel lobby where we were both having breakfast and I asked him—the way a fan would—what he was working on now. He told me that he was finishing a book called *The Reenactments,* about the making of the movie *Being Flynn*. And of course, I thought, in the same way that a mirror reflects a mirror reflects a mirror through the dizzying hall of eternity, that I was looking at Nick Flynn who wrote a book about his life that was made into a movie about his life and now was being made into a book about a movie about his life.

How odd, I remember thinking. What if nobody likes the movie? Who's going to read a book about a movie nobody liked?

But then, right after that thought came this: it didn't matter. However *The Reenactments* turned out, it will be like everything else that Nick Flynn writes—a gorgeous meditation on some newest version of Nick, living the same life he has when he is being Nick Flynn.

I Know How it Ends

In 1988, the only thing that was happening in my life was A.A. and people with AIDS. I was living in Brooklyn with an architect in a loft that had once been a picture frame factory and I was still trying to figure out what to write, now that I was coming out of the coma that had been my drinking life. I wasn't sure I could say anything with this new thinking because my only subject in those early days of not drinking was, well, not drinking. And gratitude for living, which made it so that I couldn't think of any sentences for gratitude that wouldn't be laced with syrup.

So, I read poetry, since early sobriety messes with your attention span. And once inside poetry, I wanted to read poems that talked of AIDS because my aesthetic—which hadn't been flattened by booze—knew that one of the tasks of a poem was making something lyrical out of something catastrophic. Reading had a different kind of power, one that made it feel as though I, myself, was the only way back into being a writer. Since I couldn't find any poems about AIDS, I wrote one called "Naming the Elements," about a friend who had just been diagnosed HIV-positive. And after that, Jean Valentine told me about Mark Doty's title poem from his first book, *Turtle, Swan,* which she had heard him read at her cousin's graduation from Vermont College. And so now there were two poems about AIDS.

Then I wrote a letter to a poet asking for a third poem—and I thought I might now make a book of poems about AIDS—and that poet sent a poem to me as well. And then I wrote another letter to another poet, and eventually, a desire for certainty led to a two-year project of gathering poems, culminating in an anthology called *Poets for Life: 76 Poets Respond to AIDS.*

I knew there had to be a specific response to this new way we were living, a response that could emerge as poetry, but the only thing that qualified me to put together such a book was a hunger to read something that hadn't been written yet—homesick maybe, as David Kalstone once described Elizabeth Bishop—for a place I had never been. I never thought that making a book like this was something activist in nature because the call to action was simply an innate response to what I saw as a lapse in the American collective consciousness.

One of writer Sarah Schulman's early responses to AIDS was her novel called *People in Trouble*—a book that became embroiled in a controversy that had nothing to do with the book's subject matter, but how the subject matter was later co-opted by a playwright. The novel follows a bunch of artists living in the East Village and how they live with AIDS, and with homelessness. Years later, while Michael Korie was watching a performance of Jonathan Larson's musical *Rent,* he recognized that the same essential elements of AIDS and homelessness in Schulman's novel were the same motifs recurring in Larson's musical. What made his realization even more startling was the fact that Schulman herself didn't recognize her own ideas when, weeks before, she'd been out on assignment to review the show.

"I wrote that book a long time ago," Schulman told me when all of this was coming down. "I forgot what it was about."

What Schulman did was to respond by writing a book, a far better (in her estimation) alternative than taking the Larson estate to court—particularly since this was a time she was trying to make a name for herself as a playwright.

Stagestruck is the book Sarah Schulman wrote in response—a work of non-fiction about theater and AIDS which uses the *Rent* story, according to critic Michael Bronski, "as a springboard to discuss the broader and more complex issues of how gay themes—particularly AIDS—are used and distorted in mainstream culture." The publication of *Stagestruck* was a great literary moment because Schulman knew that original ideas—those things that last in evergreen—could only arise by sitting down and writing a new book.

At its most organic, I suppose literary activism is the exact opposite of writing to get a book deal—at least in terms of the success that beginning writers seem always to be dreaming about—best sellers, huge advances—that screwy consumerism that some creative acts commodify themselves into. That kind of worldly attention isn't all that destructive, but it is not the real point of writing, which is, of course, a kind of activism.

There's a terrific story about the writer Mary McCarthy, which got curiously included in a description of a writing workshop Andre Dubus III was teaching at the Fine Arts Work Center in Provincetown many summers ago. McCarthy had just finished a manuscript—a novel—which she then promptly lost somewhere. And because this was in the days before computers, McCarthy's copy was the *only* copy. At a party she attended sometime later, someone suggested: "Why not just rewrite the whole thing again—remembering what you can along the way," or some advice to that effect.

"Oh, I couldn't do that," Mary McCarthy said, "I know how it ends."

Acknowledging such wisdom about the unknown is, in itself, activist because it shows a moral exactitude where others would see merely an impulse.

I know how it ends.

What possible reason would she have to write the same thing twice that wasn't merely administrative?

The Tricky Part is a memoir of Marty Moran's sexual awakening, which is told in fragments since its origin is in his seduction by a counselor at a Catholic church camp when he was 12. The book uses that event to unlock a myriad of longings and later became the basis of a one-man show. When Mike Nichols approached Marty to turn *The Tricky Part* into a screenplay which, ostensibly, Nichols would then direct, Marty couldn't do it. He tried to—writing dialogue, setting up the scenes, finding ideas for the camera to frame—but Marty's source material had been engaged so completely already that Marty, as an artist, couldn't see the point in going into all of it again.

I know how it ends.

If it's true, as Thomas Mann suggests, "a writer is somebody for whom writing is more difficult than it is for other people," then this is most true when a writer comes to the empty page—each time taking an aspect of being alive they hadn't considered before.

The poet Gail Mazur once ended an interview with this:

"When you finish a book, you have a really urgent desire to have your next poems be different. To leave behind whatever it is you've been doing. For some people, it's an incredible trigger. For me, it's almost been paralyzing. I almost forbid myself to worry about that anymore. I would hope that there would be more of the world, more history, more courage in them."

What the literary activist does is step outside their work, so they can read what it says.

Carnival!

(Broadway, Imperial Theatre, 1963)

I saw *Carnival!* when I was nine years old, between a mother and two fathers.

This was the year my stepfather called my father to tell him that he and my mother were taking us to live with them, and we would no longer be making weekend train rides to Connecticut to see my father and new stepmother.

I loved the theater from the beginning of time because it wasn't as confusing as life.

I once saw Anna Marie Alberghetti, who was the star of *Carnival!*, sitting at a table at Sardi's with a broken arm.

Kaye Ballard was in *Carnival!* and so was Jerry Orbach.

Kaye Ballard sang a song called "Humming," which had the lyric, "He'll be humming when I walk into that trailer," which was the first of a million songs I heard about men who don't listen to women.

On the record jacket of the original cast album of *Carnival!* there's an illustration of a woman holding a bunch of balloons that may or may not be taking her off the ground.

It's hard to tell, as there is no horizon line there.

Carnival! also had the song "Love Makes the World Go Round," which, we all know, isn't true. Power makes the world go round. Power and poverty.

I always wondered, after seeing Anna Marie Alberghetti one way in *Carnival!* and then seeing her another way at Sardi's, how it is possible that a person can eat with a broken arm—like the way, in Sherwood Anderson's short story "I Want to Know Why," a groom on the racetrack sees a trainer do something he never imagined could be part of his character.

Sunday in the Park with George

(Broadway, Booth Theatre, 1985)

A common conversation after this play, and also, after another Sondheim/Lapine collaboration, *Into the Woods,* is that Sondheim's second acts have nothing to do with the first. But this has probably more to do with the organizing aesthetic of James Lapine, who directed both musicals. Now, of course, most plays don't have either acts or intermissions. And because the cost of going to the theatre is so prohibitive, New Yorkers are being held hostage—giving a standing ovation to a mediocre production just because they paid so much money for it.

In *Sunday in the Park with George*, Bernadette Peters literally steps out of a dress on stage.

The dress stays there while she walks through the space of no dresses.

In *Sunday in the Park with George,* "Move On," another beautiful song written for the theater, talks about being an artist. Many of the songs in the musical are aimed in that direction. Sondheim likes to score rhetoric, but it never sounds dogmatic.

"Pretty isn't beautiful, mother/pretty is what changes/what the eye arranges is what is beautiful,"—a good example of Sondheim folding a message he has written and put in the hand of his leading character.

Nina Simone

The first time I heard Nina Simone was in my high school girlfriend's bedroom where a canary had gotten loose from its cage. And because Simone's sound was unlike any I'd heard before, I listened to the singing that much harder, trying to get inside of it, because, in the way it is with every great singer, everything I wanted to know about Nina Simone was in her singing. The same way that everything I wanted to know about Judy Garland was in her singing—particularly her singing "The Man That Got Away," from *A Star is Born*, which is, for me, the most glorious five minutes of a woman singing in the history of the movies.

Most women singers I had heard up till then didn't sound like Nina Simone. And her songs were so unclassifiable—of her time, certainly, but way outside of time and ahead of time, too.

Somewhere else.

Somewhere up.

Years after that, I was given the lovely accident of meeting Nina Simone. I was working as the terrace pianist at The Village Gate, providing that tinkly ambient music that people don't really listen to while they're waiting to see a performer on the club's main stage. Nina Simone had just finished a set at a time when most of her American gigs were mostly about making enough money to settle her famous debt of back taxes which hadn't paid in the '70's as protest against the war in Vietnam.

She was standing in the Gate's vestibule, smoking a cigarette, drinking a glass of wine. It was very dark and rainy outside, and the only light coming in from the street felt dimmed by the weather. Her album *Baltimore* had just been released and I asked the singer how she felt about Randy Newman, who had written the title track. She told me how gifted Newman was and how strange it was that other singers left his music alone and didn't try covering his songs. Then she asked me if the Brasserie Restaurant was still open 24 hours—the way it had been the last time she'd been in New York, some years ago. I told her that yes, it was open. And yes, the food was still bad—precisely because it *was* open 24 hours.

Nina Simone laughed.

I was alone with Nina Simone laughing.

She asked me if I wanted to go uptown and join her, but I was too shy and said no. I didn't dare break the spell that began right there, in the vestibule of a jazz club in Greenwich Village. I didn't want to change the circumstances of what brought us together.

Nina Simone gave me her empty wine glass.

I was alone with Nina Simone giving me her empty wine glass.

Then she got into the black limousine that had been waiting the whole time we were together, and I watched as she drove away. It was the first intimate moment I ever had with an artist of that stature, and instead of feeling like an unqualified nobody standing next to someone I completely idolized, another feeling surprised me. The entire time I was with her, I felt wholly like myself, like Nina Simone was somebody I already knew.

And so, with none of that intimidation and no traces of performance energy coming off the body of Nina Simone, I saw her as wholly herself—having a glass of wine, talking about Randy Newman, wanting a meal after a gig, wanting to know if that restaurant was still open.

I would never see her again.

But that night—with the Greenwich Village rain setting the scene—I like to think we saw each other the way we really are.

Kurt Elling

Of all the sentimental advisories written as lyrics in popular music, none may be truer than ...*the greatest thing that you could ever learn is to love and be loved in return*—the epiphany of the song "Nature Boy," a rendition of which is sung by the genius jazz singer Kurt Elling.

I love Kurt Elling.

Kurt Elling is the newest jazz singer that I love.

I heard him on some college radio station and have since wondered—the way I always wonder about something I love so instantly—where was I when *that* happened?

Kurt Elling will never love me in return. I know that.

We will only meet the way anyone in an audience might meet a beloved performer—in June, as it happens, when he came to New York to perform at Birdland.

Kurt Elling likes harmonies that emphasize the notes in the shadows—notes you might hear in back of those that make up the syntax of notes that make up the song. On one recording, Kurt Elling reads poetry while jazz accompanies him—like the beats used to do in the '50s.

Those were the days—jazz and poetry taking off their clothes in front of each other.

Movie Music

I once read an article in the newspaper about how the downward economy has affected artists, which was such a strange thing to be reading. It's like wondering how the downward economy has affected poor people.

Poorly, I imagine.

Poorer.

I love movie music—real movie music—music *composed* for the movie—not hip hop-or-love-song-tracks-taken-off-other-albums film music.

The music I'm talking about is written by someone who is watching the movie and writing notes for what happens to them.

That music.

I've talked about this in my chapter about influences, but I want to say more here. There were, in the '60s, two scores that simply lifted me out of my seat: Elmer Bernstein's score for *To Kill a Mockingbird* and Laurence Rosenthal's music written for *The Miracle Worker,* followed closely by Alex North's music for *Who's Afraid of Virginia Woolf?*

Both Bernstein's and Rosenthal's scores are a perfect landscape of sound for what you see on the screen. And, as it happens, the sound of the wind in those landscapes seems to be blowing through each of those themes—particularly by way of the string section, from where the dark, circular beauty of the last seasons of childhood and death of innocence are conjured.

In the opening shot of *The Miracle Worker* (directed by Arthur Penn) Patty Duke as Helen Keller is feeling her way through the wind and the grass near her home. Those were the days of black and white movies (which in itself always made film scores feel like something to be taken seriously), and that beautiful theme as the credits are rolling is a kind of lopsided waltz—a series of short, closely-voiced, three-note passages, haunting us until they resolve into a longer passage voiced in a major key.

What you are hearing, I think, is the trajectory of the film—that girl we are looking at in her black and white jumper is going to have her world break open. Before, that world was silent and dark, only sounding like a grace note before a heartbeat—that three-note phase. Her world—we know it's hers because it's Helen Keller and then we re-know this because of Laurence Rosenthal—will widen into language and evolve into a word for that thing that is cold and wet and comes from out of a well.

W-a-t-e-r. It has a sound.

Those films, with music by Bernstein and Rosenthal and North, have *their own* sound, as much as they have their own actors, their directors, their scripts. Sometimes I'll watch just the credits of those black-and-white masterpieces to hear that music. And that music might be the thing about those movies that makes me come back.

Try to make your life as though it's a movie, and you and God are going to watch it. Try to make some parts that he will like.

— Bawa Muhaiyaddeen

Michael Jeter

I had the strangest dream last night about my old friend, actor Michael Jeter, who died in 2003. We were walking on a city street—a hard-to-recognize city street because it wasn't New York and I haven't been to any other city long enough to dream about it, except the city of Newport, Rhode Island, which is where I dream now.

Michael was walking a few feet in front of me, and with each step, the sky was getting darker, and some lights started to come on from out of vague storefronts, with windows with nothing in them except stacks of construction paper. In the dream, it felt like I was with Michael—it had begun with him in some undefinable somewhere—but as the dream kept getting gradually darker, I was dream-thinking that maybe we weren't together. That maybe I was following him, or he had suddenly appeared in front of me at some beginning of the dream that I either didn't remember or never actually had.

Eventually (how long is walking in a dream, how long the haunted boulevard), Michael took some steps down into what seemed like a bar. There was a name I can't now remember above the doorway that sounded like the name of a bar.

If I owned a bar, I'd call it Eighty-Sixed or Sinister Wisdom.

Michael walked in and I walked in after him and inside was a long hallway of concrete figures resembling people sitting at a counter. I was curiously terrified and took a seat next to Michael while the bartender asked me what I wanted to drink. I actually woke myself up in the middle of answering the bartender, "I'll have a whiskey and soda, and don't be stingy," The original line, from the film, *Anna Christie* starring Greta Garbo—I remembered upon waking—was "Give me a whiskey, ginger ale on the side. And don't be stingy, baby,"

I first met Michael Jeter in New York, on the Upper West Side, at a weekly meeting of people who were trying to stay sober. He was so funny that his humor seemed more than enough to like about him without having to know anything more about him and being funny is something about a person I can catch one-handed. Michael was an actor, but at the time—like most actors in New York—he was making a living at something else, which happened to be the same thing I was making a living at—working nights as word processor at a prestigious New York law firm.

Michael would call me every now and then and soon enough asked me out on what I could only think of as a date because I could already tell he was attracted to me, more than I was attracted to him. I completely loved his mind, and maybe I should have let that love spread out and move in the direction of his body, but I was too new to sobriety to know what I was feeling half the time.

We had dinner somewhere, and on the way back to his apartment afterwards we were talking about someone we both knew who wasn't very bright and Michael said, "He's dumber than a box of hair," which was very close to the funniest thing I ever heard anybody say. It was so funny that I fell in a heap at a crosswalk on Riverside Drive. God, he was funny, which also made him angelic.

At his apartment, we talked about books we loved, and he turned me on to Nabokov, simply by pointing out what he believed was the finest sentence in literature, from *Lolita*.

> *"My very photogenic mother died in a freak accident (picnic, lightning) when I was three, and, save for a pocket of warmth in the darkest past..."*

I had hot flashes during Michael's reading of that to me and probably should have kissed him right then and there. But I left. And then I only saw him one more time before he moved to California. He'd gotten a role in the new Tommy Tune musical, *Grand Hotel*, based on the Greta Garbo classic. In an extraordinary demonstration of kindness, Michael got tickets for a big group of us to see the show and then he took us all out to dinner afterwards. Later that year, he would win a Tony Award for his performance and give an acceptance speech that remains one of the most moving acceptance speeches ever given by an actor. Then he left New York and eventually died from AIDS in California.

I remember being so angry at his death—sad, of course, but mad at thinking—true or not—that if he had only stayed in New York, and

HIV-negative, Michael wouldn't have seroconverted and eventually died from the disease. On top of that, I never saw Michael as a California kind of guy, but a New Yorker through and through. His humor and intelligence were too radiant to ever be appreciated by people in the West. His one performance as a homeless drag queen in the film *The Fisher King*, delivering a telegram to an office worker while belting out a hysterical, seminal rendition of "Rose's Turn" from *Gypsy*, was Jeter genius, and still my favorite image of him—pure joy, pure nobody else like him in the world.

As I'm writing this, the sky is slowly darkening the way it did in my weird dream about Michael, and I've been trying to figure out all day—in that strange way a dream you remember keeps remembering you in the daylight hours—what all of it meant.

The concrete and the dark? What did they mean?

Michael, of all people, to begin with?

But like every dream, the meaning, the secret of the dream, is lost the more you try to figure it out.

Michael came to visit me in a city neither of us had ever been to, and I woke myself up laughing about a drink order, wishing he had come with me, out of the dream, into the light he had disappeared into.

Slumdog Millionaire

Some years ago, I found myself going to the movies a lot—a lot for me, anyway—for married me. When I was single, I used to go to the movies all the time because that's what single people do. Single people go to the movies, eat in restaurants, read, smoke cigarettes, and drink coffee. And, occasionally, for me anyway, single people have sex with other people who are also, but not always, single. For me, single men. I also had pretty regular sex with a married man, but I don't think his other man ever actually existed—at least not in New York, not living in a New York apartment. Still, he was, to be sure, very much alive in the married man's mind.

The life of the mind is very much at play in *Slumdog Millionaire*, which is good but not great. The movie is very vibrant and includes many extraordinary exterior shots of Mumbai, India, which is where the people in the movie live. And there seems to be paint peeling off everything in sight. And lots of crowds—everywhere you look—even on the television, where the indelible events of the contestant's life aid him on *Who Wants to be a Millionaire* in winning a great deal of money.

The sublime quality here is that all the answers to the questions relate supernaturally and specifically to the events of his incredible past, in which he learned how to survive against the most varied and horrific of odds. It's a movie about surviving the story as a way of remembering the story.

Seamlessly made. Wonderful soundtrack.

Goofy Hollywood ending—kissing—which is such an empty ending and so trite it almost washes away with sanitizer the story that came before it. Kissing at the end of a movie is just letting all the colors of the film run together into a happy mass of gladness.

People Are Funny

When I had a day job I never told anybody that I was a writer because most of the people I worked with didn't read—not literature, anyway—and for someone to announce he's a writer, much less a poet, to someone who doesn't read, is like saying you're queer to someone who doesn't have sex.

The other reason I didn't tell people that I'm a writer is that I didn't want them to think I haven't succeeded as one. With all the other work I have to do, just finishing a book feels like success because it takes so long to write one amid all the interruptions. But I'm not in a hurry to get books into the world. Writers who are in a hurry, I've noticed, tend to write the same book twice. And besides all that, I was really bad at blowing my own horn. But that was then. I'm older and crankier now and have just—with a new book of poems published last year—gotten better at the trumpet.

I think the trumpet has something to do with not knowing what's good about me. I mean, even if I was somewhat pleased with my work (and one should never be totally pleased with one's work, unless one is making jewelry or throwing pots) I wouldn't talk about it because talking about it can talk the writing away and I would rather people read what I have to say. Unless I am thinking of something funny, in which case I would rather have people hear what I have to say because I'm not a particularly funny writer, which is too bad because I LOVE funny. Funny anything. But especially funny people.

The woman from work, also a writer, was talking about time and how rare it is to put toward writing.

She's telling me, "I have to cobble fragments of time together in order to get any writing done, especially when you have three jobs like I do."

Then, out of the blue she asks me, "Do you have any kids?"

"No," I tell her. "I don't have kids, I'm gay."

And she says, "Oh, that doesn't matter, you could still have kids," as if she were telling me something I didn't know or never considered—as if her sole purpose in this moment was to liberate me from the bondages of my internalized homophobia.

I could have continued the conversation about gay people and children and what I think about the two together or independently of each other, but I just didn't have the energy or any real interest in traveling down that road. I confess, I really am one of those homosexuals who secretly—when I know God and I are alone—believes that part of the reason he's queer is because he never wanted to have kids—which means he doesn't want to have the kind of sex that could lead to kids—which means not having sex—because this is Earth—with women.

It wasn't a conscious choice, for me, of course. I didn't wake up one day and conclude that, because I liked having the occasional penis somewhere I could or couldn't see, it meant that I didn't qualify as someone who could be a father, even if he wanted to. My contribution to the world would not involve making people, but making something else—like a poem, for instance—whenever life decides to strike the hot anvil of love.

The Money Job

Somebody once asked Grace Paley if she had any advice for someone who wanted to be a writer, and without even thinking, she responded: "Have a low overhead." It's great advice—especially for those poor souls dazzled into thinking they can make big money as a writer—but I've never taken it. I survive, even thrive, no matter how much money is coming in because I've never been someone who only writes. And still, five books of poetry and two memoirs were written while day jobs covered the overhead.

Many years ago, when I knew my heart was with poetry, I was keenly aware that I would also have to get a job. Poetry isn't something you do for the money (even if you make money doing it, which is exceedingly rare). But I also wanted a job because, honestly, I couldn't bear the idea of living with poetry all day—making it, reading it, teaching it, thinking about it. I've always admired those for whom poetry is a true vocation, like William Stafford, who in his workmanlike way was engaged every day with vision and revision. But for me, I've never had the temperament or skill of somebody who can sit at a desk every day with a restless heart and pursue the empty page.

I get antsy. I need a break. After exalted periods with poems, thinking starts to feel occult. And occasionally, something even worse happens. I completely lose the thread of language and what it does and what I am doing with it that hasn't been done before.

For me, a day job is a break from writing as much as it is a necessary activity that has nothing to do with writing. And like many writers, I've had a number of different jobs: line worker at a factory, fry cook, taxi driver, typesetter, groom, and, for three years, a faculty member at Sarah Lawrence College. But even with the teaching, I usually also had a job as a legal assistant at various law firms in New York.

At that last job, I was under some pressure because I worked in one of the country's leading intellectual property departments (trademark infringement and counterfeiting), which has the blood of deadlines and government filing running through its veins. The work was always concerned with theft or misrepresentation of someone's original idea; it has a lot of moving parts. We staged raids in New York State or California or Texas and confiscated counterfeit shoes, perfume, and sweatshirts.

Every day, I would write cease and desist letters to alleged counterfeiters and trademark infringers and search the internet to see if anyone was using the word *vagabond* on a T-shirt, because our high-profile client wanted to put it on theirs. There were deadlines to oppose a competitor's trademark application should it be too close to the one our client was already composing. And there were phone calls from online Chinese counterfeiters asking in broken English why we'd frozen their PayPal accounts.

I liked the job because it was varied and precise and it kept me in the world of proof instead of the vague, narcissistic world, with my worth as a writer circling inside it. I also don't mind—and I don't know where this comes from, exactly—working for other people. I like getting paid on a schedule. And I'm at the age where I need health insurance more than I once did, and having a job provides that mercurial security, coming at a price I could never afford, were I uncertain where the next freelance writing assignment or teaching gig would come from.

Most important, the job allowed me the freedom to write exactly what I pleased without worrying if it would put food on my plate. I know people who spend a significant portion of their days waiting for the next writing assignment or advance on a book deal. There's a disposition of hunger that settles like a habit onto that kind of writer; it eventually resembles the weird vibration of an addict looking for a fix, looking hungry, because that's what they are.

In those days, I had to pay for a car, insurance, and two mortgages, so I supplemented my income from the law firm by teaching at Goddard's low-residency MFA program, using my vacation time from my law job to attend the required residences twice a year. But I didn't think of my teaching as a job, because teaching puts the mind closer to the place where writing comes from—closer than, say, waiting tables, figuring out the state tax on a dinner check, or, if you are following in the footsteps of William Carlos Williams's, examining the next patient.

In addition to being a revolutionary figure in American poetry, Williams was a pediatrician—famously known for writing poems on prescription pads or on a typewriter that fit inside the well of his desk, one he could stick away whenever he had a patient. These breaks, of course, gave his poems the quality of one line stacked on top of the next—a poem interrupted—since that's exactly what happened. He kept coming back to the line he had last written between his appointments with the world.

Every writer who has had a day job—a money job, a survival job—has had such appointments. Before her debut story collection, *Bad Behavior*, was published in 1988, Mary Gaitskill was a proofreader at one of the law firms where I worked. A good buddy of mine at that time, the novelist Ryan Boudinot wrote his first two books at night, during the years he worked for Amazon and Expedia, after he put the kids to bed. T.S. Eliot was a clerk; Wallace Stevens was an insurance claims adjuster. Kafka, a lawyer.

Both my parents worked all the time (my mother in publishing, my stepfather in law), but having jobs didn't mean that they knew anything about money. My stepfather was a compulsive gambler and watching him win and lose encouraged something in me opposite to anything in his makeup: a strong work ethic arrived at by working for a living, or, more precisely, thinking about where the money was going to come from. Because being the stepson of a compulsive gambler meant there was no fiscal responsibility in the family. Although my mother worked, I always sensed that she spent all the money she made on herself. In many ways I still don't know what making a living actually is; I survive, like a lot of artists, from paycheck to paycheck and sometimes from windfall to windfall—particularly with horses, when stake races were run, and I got a percentage of the purse.

But money and being an artist have never seemed connected to me, nor do I think they should be. Of course, I envy the "successful" writers: the ones who get up each and every day and walk the short distance to the room in which they work or to the studio apartment they bought years ago to live in and can now afford to keep solely as an office. I envy anyone whose time is utterly their own.

But I also know—long-recovering alcoholic that I am, who believed his sponsor when he told him that a problem in early sobriety is how to figure out what to do with unstructured time—that I need the structured time that comes with a day job. The space I used to saturate with liquor now fills up with work, with action.

Does having a day job make me less of an artist than someone whose day unfolds like another sunny desert island to inhabit? Probably. But whatever I do as an artist is the result of every job I've ever had. And I seriously doubt I would get more writing done if I didn't have some kind of money-job. I would most likely find something else to distract me—some life charm to draw me away from staring too closely at the face of that demanding demon/angel too lightly named the Muse. What I have never lost track of in all my clocked-in hours is the ability to recognize beauty in even the most mundane encounters, and how beauty enlarges the world when it gets entangled with language.

There's a famous and very funny story about the Broadway production of *I Hate Hamlet*, in which, during rehearsals, its star, Nicol Williamson, kept striking another actor, Evan Handler, with a foil during a fencing scene. Williamson would not stop hitting his fellow actor, even when he was told repeatedly to knock it off. One night, Handler had had enough and told Williamson that if it happened again, he'd walk off the stage. And, of course, it happened again on opening night. And as promised, Handler promptly exited the stage, at which point a semi-horrified Williamson spun around and faced the audience and plaintively asked, "Well, should I sing?"

It's a funny story, assuming he could sing (and even funnier if he couldn't), but it also makes me wonder how I would react if I, like the actor left to rely on this whole other talent, once his acting partner exited the stage, were to be laid off or fired—especially now, in this anti-economy.

"Well, what should I do now? Write?"

Well, of course, I would write. But I would also—because I'm that kind of writer—look for a job.

Ghost Town

I watched *Ghost Town* on DVD last night. The one thing this movie proves is that Ricky Gervais is a master of understatement. He reminds me of Buster Keaton the way his face expresses so much with so little movement. It's one of those movies (the more popular *The Sixth Sense* is like this, too) where someone can see dead people. But the movie kept making me think of better ghost stories, like *Topper* or *The Uninvited*. In those movies, the dead are palpable and still find things wondrous about inhabiting a body. In those movies, dead people are just people who didn't finish living, and in this movie, they are still only thinking of themselves.

Narcissistic ghosts. What an oxymoron.

Aren't ghosts transparent because the ego has left like a bird out the window?

Movies were king when they glimpsed life without end.

Think: Shangri-La.

American Utopia

(Broadway, Hudson Theatre, 2019)

Joan Baez once described bliss as dancing barefoot in a church.

My bliss, which I can easily forget living in this surrealistic republic, returned to life a few years ago in a Broadway theater.

In *American Utopia*, David Bryne is beautifully suited in gray, preparing to slide from stage left to stage right in his bare feet, which can be interpreted as sliding into another view of America. He is being followed—no, *charmed*—by his band of Americans and American immigrants suited in gray, similarly hitting the stage barefooted and playing instruments of percussion.

The curtain—designed by the immediately identifiable artist Maira Kalman—rises on David Byrne sitting at a table meditating on a life-size replica of a human brain, as though it were an artifact—which, after A.I.'s gotten through with us—it will be.

David Byrne is giving us a little lecture about those famous regions of gray matter—those parts of gray matter that send light to the rest of the body. And he says that when we're born, our brains are working at full capacity but lessen over time. We begin in enlightenment.

American Utopia is, in part, a post-woke dream inspired by a phenomenological brain. Bryne's crackerjack band of percussive misfits seems to have found the secret to getting their baby brain back.

What would a whole world of adult babies look like? Could there ever be war? What if we could all get those lost electrodes back?

Through every draft I wrote of what you are reading here, it became increasingly difficult for me to find a language exact enough to describe how achingly beautiful and humane *American Utopia* is. And it also feels strange to be happy about something, anything—like this artifact of an artifact.

I saw the second performance of Stephen Sondheim's masterpiece, *Sweeney Todd: The Demon Barber of Fleet Street*, and up until *American*

Utopia, that had been the best night I ever had at the theater. *Sweeney Todd* was especially surprising as a musical—electrifying. The score alone was more ravishing than that of any other musical, including other Sondheim musicals. The story was a murderous one. But at its heart, it was political theater, with the same kind of urgent, activist fire.

Who gets to eat? And who gets eaten?

What Byrne and his merry band of mavericks were doing on stage was the theatrical equivalent of group-think hypnosis—constructing an experience inspired by the brain's desire to be found again, in order to save a dying planet.

Will the world end before we have a chance to?

How can we reclaim the electricity in the human brain that first enlightened us?

Byrne faces living and dying with a childlike reverence—a facet, I'm certain, of his being on the autistic spectrum.

One song was a rhapsody about how looking at the human face is the best thing to look at in all the world—better than, say, a colorful bag of popcorn or a beautiful sunset. Byrne's genius is coupling his singularity with a restless and curious humility, humility and—I would have to say—his resistance to even a whisper of sentimentality.

Every day in these waning days of empire is another day to think about what an army of activists, artists and scientists, academics, and brilliant young people would look like. It could very well be, as it has been written, that a child will lead them. I'm longing for the force of humanity to slip without fanfare inside the force of nature, to advocate for a worldwide will intent on saving the planet, and ourselves. Who is ready, among us, to bring the world *to* life and not more dead?

David Byrne is giving us a look, in his documentary of music and dance, into what joy looks like.

I want everything his band is singing about.

I want to join the tribe that goes barefoot—to touch the earth in a gray suit.

I want to walk out with them, the children, and the makers, far from the tiresome ridicules of empire.

And leap the way children leap into an everyday miracle.

Boredom and Artificial Intelligence

It's inconceivable to me that Toni Morrison's masterpiece, *Beloved,* is banned in some places in America. This isn't just an insult to the book and to the writer, it's also a misconception of what book banning is really about—banning the imagination.

Right now in America the real news is that we are funding wars and banning books.

For now.

Let's say someone is to be given a lethal injection because they're on death row for a crime, let's say, that they didn't commit. And that person is asked if s/he has any last words and s/he says, "I'm innocent," and then s/he says something like—and this is the arrow heading for the point I'm making here, "You can take my life, but you will never take away my freedom."

Well, that's what we're doing here in America.

For now.

In a strange shift, one accelerated in the last couple of years—the American citizenry is having their inalienable rights picked off one by one. You know the list. I don't have to bore you with the list—the banality of it. I keep my list on my refrigerator because I keep having to add to it.

At the same time, A.I. rushes in like the messiah.

I'm not a fan, but I could be if artificial intelligence were used to put an end to some of our human unsolveables—like stress, like racism, like war.

Famous poet and jumbo shrimp, to cite just two examples, are oxymorons.

So is artificial intelligence.

If intelligence is an aspect of being human, as well as of some other living things, like dogs and animals that know how to migrate, sometimes over such long and weary distances, then it follows that artificial intelligence is one aspect of … what?

One aspect of what it means to be artificial?

Is this our fourth encounter of the close kind with extraterrestrial life?

What is A.I.'s endgame? Six horsemen?

A.I. at its artificially worst: WRITE A NOVEL IN FIVE DAYS!!!

Why on earth would anyone want to write a novel in five days, unless there was a gun pointed at their head? Apart from the pleasure of inventing a story and its characters and writing dialogue and considering diction and inhabiting all that as a world-in-making, the hard joy of writing a novel is the simple bounty of time—the time it takes—however long it takes—to finish one.

I have never heard a writer say, "Man, that book just took way too long to write!" Because it always takes a long time to write a book, unless A.I. wrote it.

But artificial intelligence will never be able to write a poem because to write a poem, the creator has to be intelligent *and* wonderstruck.

Artificial intelligence doesn't deal in wonder. It is a shredder and recombiner of human ideas.

It does not create. It replicates. Which will eventually make it hard to see what the world really looks like.

A.O. Scott wrote an essay called "Literature Under the Spell of A.I." But this title isn't accurate. Literature isn't under the spell of A.I.. A.I. is under the spell of literature.

If Literature were under the spell of A.I., agents would have been replaced by robots.

A.O. Scott's subtitle to the essay is: "*What Happens When Writers Embrace Artificial Intelligence as Their Muse.*" This is also incorrect for the same reason his primary title is inaccurate. A.I. is embracing writers as *its* muse. This is why my friend Matt Klam and other writers took an A.I. sweatshop to court.

Lily Tomlin said, in her one-woman show, during the golden age of intelligent people being invited to the White House, that she hoped whoever invented Muzak wasn't thinking up something else.

Ditto A.I.

But what is there after A.I.?

A.O. Scott's essay, referring to a chatbot-generated novella entitled "Death of an Author" says, "My colleague Dwight Garner described it,

perhaps generously, as 'arguably the first halfway readable A.I. novel.'"
Arguably?! Halfway readable?!

I'm prickly at the thought of reading an A.I. novel because one of the pleasures of reading is listening to all its different voices. I couldn't get through a book, I don't think, that was written in, say, the monotone voice of HAL 9000—that crazy, lovable, intelligent computer star of *2001: A Space Odyssey.*

Do you remember what happened to HAL at the end of the movie? He went mad because he couldn't tell the difference between what the crew needed to know and what should be kept confidential.

I think in a worst case scenario, at some point in a future that feels nearer than we ever could have imagined, A.I. won't be able to tell the difference between love and fear.

Read at whim.

—Randall Jarrell

Wall-E

I saw *Wall-E* last night because it's on Blu-ray and Andrew and I got ourselves a Blu-ray disc player for Christmas since the DVD player that came built inside the TV we bought a few years ago stopped working after Andrew slipped a broken DVD between its lips. He didn't know it was broken. Anyway, Blu-Ray is kind of great (but how much clearer can anything truly get?) Eventually, crystal-clear always makes me long for the out of focus world of the morning before I can find my glasses or the out of focus photographs of John Dugdale.

Wall-E is a lovely and virtually silent love story about earth and robots and annihilation. And it's about the gluttonous eventuality of consumerism. It's amazing to look at—the way that anything Pixar is amazing to look at because they discovered how to make animation as pictorially various as reality. *Wall-E* is also a movie about an unlikely savior: the movie musical.

Weirdly and exhilaratingly, the song "Put on Your Sunday Clothes" from *Hello Dolly* (the film version, not the terrific Jerry Dodge rendition from the original Broadway cast) opens *Wall-E*. It plays during the opening credits over a long shot of starry space. Later, when we see the visual that matches the song on a battered video tape, it feels like an elegy for a civilization that once sang and danced. Of all the things to remember about what life on earth must have been like before robots took over, I'm sure there is nothing as sublime as the movie musical.

I remember the thrill I felt after the first time I saw *That's Entertainment*—singing and dancing at its most vital and memorable—and thinking then that this would be the film the next civilization would look at to judge, at our best, who we were.

Wall-E knows this, too.

Harvey Milk and Galen McKinley

In the song, "There Won't be Trumpets," from Stephen Sondheim's chaotic musical, *Anyone Can Whistle*, there's a lyric that goes, "... *a hero doesn't come till the nick of time!*" And whenever I hear Lee Remick sing that song I think of Harvey Milk and Larry Kramer—men whose fight was a way of staying in love with the world while never losing sense of what was so clearly wrong with it. Harvey Milk was a great reminder for people who, at that time, didn't realize that gay rights and human rights were inseparable. Maybe the term human rights is ironically overused in a world that is still confused about its meaning. Don't human beings—by nature of their humanness—already have rights? Inalienable rights?

I knew Harvey Milk through stories told to me by Galen McKinley, who had been one of Harvey's ex-lovers. When I met Galen in the '70's, he was a stage manager for the first revival on Broadway of Tom O'Horgan's *Hair*—a show I auditioned for and was hired to understudy for the role of Claude (but only if I went on tour with the German company, which I couldn't imagine doing, for reasons I forget now).

Tom and Galen worked a lot together—particularly at La Mama—which is where they first met. But like all love stories, there are conflicting reports about how exactly they did meet. In any case, they broke up after a while. And it was a bad break-up, according to Galen. And in many ways, the lasting and haunting effects of that badness kept Galen out of any long-term relationship for as long as I knew him—which, as it turned out, were the last years of his life.

When Harvey was assassinated, Galen was devastated: drinking more, tricking more—his nightlife of choice—paid homage to by naming his dog Trick. Mostly out of work by then, he finally did manage to get a job designing a single row of spotlights for Dawn Hampton in a Cuban gay bar in Hell's Kitchen called Tijuana Cat, a place where Richard, my boyfriend at the time, was bartender and where Galen, Richard, and I ended up most days of the week in an alcoholic huddle together—wheeling home in the early morning to the two slums we lived in that were connected by a postage-stamp sized courtyard on West 47th Street.

I suppose it was at the edge of one of those walks home, when the slow encompassing dawn made me feel a little more sober, that I fell a little in love with Galen McKinley. He was a force of nature before anybody called anybody a force of nature—impulsive, hysterical, gorgeous, sloppy, distracted, and inspired. And I've never stopped thinking about him. And I've never met anyone since that remotely resembles him.

Harvey Milk had been the love of Galen McKinley's life and when Harvey went, Galen was close behind. One night, a little more than a year after Harvey Milk died, Galen got drunk and started fooling around on the ledge on one of Tom O'Horgan's loft windows—eight floors up—that looked down on University Place. And Galen fell. He died at the age of 33, on February 14th, 1980. Valentine's Day.

We scattered some of Galen's ashes in the Hudson River in New York City and some of them were scattered off the Golden Gate Bridge in San Francisco, where Harvey's had been scattered the year before. Harvey and Galen were together again in the waters of the cities they came to love when alone. And without each other.

Let the Right One In

What an amazing, strange, and tender love story this Swedish vampire movie, *Let the Right One In,* is, directed by Tomas Alfredson. It's finally out on DVD in this country (after being released in its Swedish close to its theatrical release last year) and the quality here is swell. In some ways the film reminds me of Krzysztof Kieslowski's profoundly moving series, *Decalogue,* made for Polish television. There's a similar bleakness made up of the night (day, or the reminders of day, only come in flashes) and of the snow. Snow, especially.

Let the Right One In is about Eli, a 12-year-old girl vampire (and as androgynous a one as a horror flick can allow), who has been 12 years old for more than 200 years. She falls in love with Oskar, the blond dreamer who the bullies at the school target because he's unreadable—a screen on which to project bully-angst upon.

Oskar lives with his mother in the creepy apartment complex and sees his father (vaguely queer) only on what we can assume are the weekends, which is hard to tell, because every day in the movie feels the same.

Eli lives with someone like a father, though we're never really sure what the relationship is because from the beginning we sense the father is on some kind of mission.

That mission, as it turns out, is to kill people, hang them upside down and drain their blood so that Eli can live. Eventually—and importantly—Eli has to fend for herself, and Oskar is slowly made aware of the extraordinary and complex and truly otherworldly world he has entered. But the horror in that world is muffled and neutralized, so that every bloody and terrible encounter (and they are prolifically shown, this is still very much in the horror genre) is flat and almost ordinary in its rhythm. Each murder is languorous, more suited to a sleepwalker than a killer, finally creating an alternate universe where people actually want to live.

Lorenz Hart

In 1939, when my mother was seven years old, the lyricist Lorenz Hart gave her a photograph of himself on which he had inscribed in midnight blue ink: "For Kathryn Jacqueline, from Lorenz Hart, whose name will probably be forgotten by the time she is able to read this." Hart had been a friend of my grandfather's, a vaudevillian. I remember reading the inscription for the first time and thinking what an extraordinary thing it was for someone to say to a child—as if childhood held the same kind of unpredictability and loneliness that fame did and that my mother could understand all that.

After my mother died in 1977, I inherited the photograph and sold it to an autograph dealer on 18th Street for drinking money.

In the museum of saddest things I've ever done, that may be the saddest. It felt like I was making fun of beauty.

Back to Getting Back to the Garden

In 1969, I was 15 years old and my progressive parents (read: young, smart, drug addled) bought me and my brother tickets for Woodstock—the music and art fair of 1969. Originally announced as "An Aquarian Exposition," it took place at Max Yasgur's 600-acre dairy farm in Bethel, New York, after the promoters couldn't find a location for the festival in the town of Woodstock itself, a more well-known haven for musicians at the time.

Could there have been other parents like my parents? Is it even possible to imagine anybody can be like anybody else's parents, who actually bought tickets to this thing that felt bigger than the world? For something that big, it seems like nobody should need a ticket. And that first day, as if by divine intervention, no ticket was needed, thanks to the crowd of us knocking over the protective fence. Then M.C. Chip Monck announced within minutes over the loudspeaker: "It's a free concert from now on. But what it means is that these people have it in their heads that your welfare is a hell of a lot more important than a dollar."

That announcement changed everything. It marked the beginning of recognizing something beyond us, turning almost half a million people into something impossible—a community made small enough to hear announcements read over a loudspeaker. We were huge, but we were local.

I recently watched the Netflix documentary, *Trainwreck: Woodstock '99*, about a people-wreck, when the safety of human beings was not a concern for the promoters, who were hoping to strike lightning a third time (the first reboot was "Woodstock '94;" "Woodstock," as a concept, seemed now to be only a trademark).

At the '99 edition, hundreds of people complained about vendors running out of the overly priced food and water. Rapes and other kinds of sexual assault were reported, and more violence erupted in pockets of crazies towards the end of the concert—mostly centered on destroying the stage and its surroundings. And as if that weren't enough, fires erupted across the expanse of what previously had been a decommissioned military base in Rome, New York. The site looked like a war zone and the seemingly mostly white male population glared into cameras like ravaged zombies, dancing wildly on the edge of their improvisational apocalypse.

What gave the first Woodstock its renown was the fact that it was, above anything else, a first. Any first has a sense of the extraordinary about it, and you claim it as either an object of devotion or ruin: first kiss, first death, first real anything. We were so many people with the same outer experience in real time that, for many of us, the entire experience was suffused with the spirit of Joni Mitchell's prescient advice to get ourselves back to the garden.

When had we seen this much humanity come together for a common cause, outside of marching that year and the year before against the war in Vietnam? Woodstock confirmed that music itself, along with the protests in the streets, was the conduit through which we, the counterculture, were being taught to listen. That—and the music was a call to rise up against the machine, the establishment's way of doing things, which clearly wasn't working.

That music was responsible for an eight-hour delay on the New York Thruway, between the city and the concert site, causing the *New York Post* to proclaim on its front page: TRAFFIC UPTIGHT AT HIPPIE FEST.

There are so many ways of being with other people when you are making history, especially when you have just lived through the previous year's history-making murders of Martin Luther King and Robert F. Kennedy—assassinations that underlined the atrocious and astonishing fact that our peacekeepers were the threat, and not the solution, to living in peace.

—

It was about the music, and it wasn't about the music.

It was about people who had tickets and about people who didn't have tickets. And then it was *really* about the people who didn't have tickets.

It was about a new friend named Licorice crawling out of her tent at 7:00 a.m. on the second day and shouting, "Does anyone have any dope to smoke?"

It was about five different voices, male and female, saying, "Over here, over here, over here, over here, over here." And not one person saying, no.

It was about the music, and it wasn't about the music.

It was about nobody saying no to anything except the rain for four days.

It was about Swami Satchidananda coming out to bless us.

It was about the artisans with their crafts setting up little shops in the woods, seeming to appear only at night in a grove I couldn't find a second time, lit up by tiny lights in the branches.

It was about those-were-the-days of the VW bus. And the couple on the third night who were braided together in a sleeping bag underneath the bus and my brother pissing on them because it was too dark to see them.

It was about not remembering money.

It was about the rain and the rains that came on August 17th. And then it was about the mudslides.

It was about searching and finding the people we were looking for.

It was about the first time in so many lifetimes that what was happening held a kind of power we were certain would be enough to rock the world—rock it back to steady.

It was about the fact that there was only one general store within walking distance, and it ran out of supplies before Ritchie Havens' opening act was finished.

It was about the drugs everywhere and how the drugs relaxed the crowd into all of us having the same high, and how I didn't hear one argument the entire time I was there.

It was about the almost otherworldly beauty of naked men and women covered in gray mud and yellow flowers singing in a nearby pond.

It was about the watermelon truck we saw whizz by and, as if, by our sheer collective will, a few dozen watermelons rolled off the truck into the road.

It was about a stranger from Little Rock, Arkansas, who had a jug of Thorazine for people who were having a bad trip.

It was about Chip Monck announcing again, saying to steer clear of the brown acid because it wasn't any good.

And about another announcement: "Helen Savage, please call your father at the Motel Glory in Woodridge." And hearing those words in Chip's musical voice: *Motel Glory.*

It was about the music, and it wasn't about the music.

It was about being lucky enough to be fed brown rice and honey by the Hog Farm and then camping out next to The Merry Pranksters, even if Ken Kesey wasn't with them that trip.

It was about watching Joan Baez rehearse on stage at 4 a.m. while only about 30 of us were awake and how we were all very quiet, standing there in the field of sleeping co-conspirators.

—

Michael Wadleigh's Oscar-winning documentary of the event really does capture the authenticity of what happened at Woodstock and perfectly documents what occurred behind the scenes, too. And then, of course, there's Joni Mitchell's anthem, "Woodstock," written in absentia, which sees the whole experience as a mega-celebration by a counterculture resolutely posed against violence, where "the bombers riding shotgun in the sky… were turning into butterflies …"

Even now, I feel such gratitude for being given that immense, but somehow still secret place, to hear so much music. That music, in such a stardust time, was the best thing about being alive in America.

Of Thee I Sing

Every day I wake up with a song in my head and join in with my own singing while stumbling into the kitchen for a cup of coffee that Andrew, in his completely wondrous way of daily life, has set to brew at the same time every morning. Which is too early.

And in the years of trying to mine this song-in-the-head phenomenon (I know the term is earworm, but it's too icky for the lyric note I'm trying to sing here), mine it for its meaning and/or occult properties (is the song like a dream a prediction of something?), I still haven't been able to figure out where these morning songs come from or what they're trying to tell me. I don't think I've ever heard music or someone singing in a dream, so the daylit songs aren't carryovers in that way.

But because it's music, I don't ask questions.

Music is like unconditional love. And a song doesn't want you to do anything except listen to it.

In an extraordinary speech given by Karl Paulnack, pianist and Director of the Music Division at Ithaca College, addressing the parents of incoming freshmen at Boston Conservatory at Berklee, he said this:

> "The Greeks said that music and astronomy were two sides of the same coin. Astronomy was seen as the study of relationships between observable, permanent, external objects, and music was seen as the study of relationships between invisible, internal, hidden objects. Music has a way of finding the big, invisible moving pieces inside our hearts and souls and helping us figure out the position of things inside us."

Of course, my navel-gazing about these songs in my head feels almost insulting in its self-servitude after reading something like this. But there is a connection to me, which is why I am quoting Paulnack, to not only call forth the mysterious in music but also to justify that mystery.

And when he says, "Music has a way of finding the big, invisible moving pieces inside our hearts and souls and helping us figure out the position of things inside us," he's describing that precise moment when, in the body, a piece of music has located the exact emotion that fosters its claim on the listener, giving it a private life. And it seems to me that in the same way we all experience reality in different ways, we also hear music in different ways, too. And when I say *hearing,* I'm not simplifying what is, of course, a *listening* experience, but we hear music before we listen to it, in the way we look before we *see.*

Many of the songs in my head are literal recordings—i.e., they seem to be set off by words that I heard on the radio, in a speech or report from the street, on television, or in a movie. Or they may be literal in terms of an object recently observed: cars, flowers, little boxes, little boxes. And a lot of them are love songs, because I love something or somebody.

The only annoying thing that happens with a song in the head is that sometimes it's a song I don't like and can't imagine how it ever got in there. Of course, it's usually a result of the song's stubbornness—its too familiar chord progression, or its incessant play on the radio, etc., etc., that causes some *sound* mirror in me to capture the bad song and sing it back to my mind. That bad song then only reminds me that I'm a consumer when I like to think of myself as a connoisseur.

Maestro

I'm so weary of all the negativity I've been reading, with a mixture of anger and fascination, in reviews of Bradley Cooper's film *Maestro*—most of which is based on some bizarre wish fulfillment people have (including critics like the scatterbrained resident oddball, Richard Brody at *The New Yorker*) about what a biography is, or should be, instead of seeing the film for what it really is—a memoir—which can be defined, in this example, as a record of how one artist looks at another artist's life. This means it's a movie about Leonard Bernstein only as much as it is about Bradley Cooper's interpretation of periods from Bernstein's life that interest him as a filmmaker, and as an artist.

The bigger issue here is why the movie isn't considered a work of art, when all of its elements (the acting, the writing, the photography, the music), clearly and lushly send the film up into the realm of art. In the opening seconds of *Maestro*, Cooper was smart to put on the screen a quote from Bernstein, which, when you consider of its frenzied reception, brilliantly answers the question people resisting the film don't know how to ask. "A work of art does not answer questions, it provokes them, and its essential meaning is in the tension between the contradictory answers."

When I was a writing teacher—and particularly when we were discussing poetry—I would urge my students to come to each poem as an empty slate. That any meaning—and hungry youth are always looking for "meaning"—could be found in front of them—not underneath the words, not with interpretation, but *in* the words the poet chose to put in their particular order. Syntax, in this way, overrides subtext. Besides, a poem already arrives as its subtext.

Any discussion of a poem after it has been written should be about what is happening to the language in front of a reader—not about what they may subjectively construe as missing. Not, i.e., "But I want to know more about the mother." Poetry isn't about what we want to know, or worse, what we already know, but about looking in a place where we haven't looked before.

So, *Maestro* has become a cultural battle cry for what it *should* have been, for what it's missing, and not for what it is—a collaboration between two artists. In this way, every negative critique gives sustenance to the void. And having been afforded the luxury of knowing quite a bit about Leonard Bernstein before seeing Cooper's film (his sexuality, the Black Panther Party get together, his cigarettes), I wasn't looking for any of that to be played out in a cinematic way, precisely because I knew some parts of Bernstein's life just wouldn't play well *reenacted*—a word, by its very definition, that lowers the stakes.

I wanted the Bernstein I didn't, or more precisely, couldn't know in any other way than in a movie by Bradley Cooper called *Maestro*. Which, among its many rewards, has as its focal point the mysterious joy that Bernstein embodies in those moments of conducting—how those moments utterly change his physical presence into something primal, the music rolling through him with invention. We can't look away from him, while also knowing there is something about genius, something triumphantly ephemeral, that we'll never see.

Writing is so hard. Why would you be a writer if you weren't really good at it?

    —Fran Lebowitz

Adrienne Rich

This might be inaccurate, but since her death in Santa Cruz on March 27th, 2012, there hasn't been a moment of any day when a spark of something Adrienne Rich said in a poem or in a letter suddenly comes to me and she's here again. The other day it was a line from a poem called "To the Days": *A cat drinks from a bowl of marigolds—his moment.*

Today, I was thinking about a visit I had with Adrienne and her partner Michelle Cliff on the deck of their house at the end of July of 1997 and telling me how this was the same month she had famously turned down President Clinton's National Medal of the Arts. In a letter addressed to Jane Alexander, then-director of the NEA, Adrienne wrote, "The very meaning of art, as I understand it, is incompatible with the cynical politics of this administration."

Then, perhaps in an effort to lighten the mood, Adrienne told me a story about Maurice Sendak, who had accepted a medal the same year. According to Adrienne, Clinton whispered in Sendak's ear, "When I was a child in Hope, Arkansas, all I really wanted do when I grew up was to be a doorman," to which Sendak snapped back, "Well, you can only be President for four more years. You can still be a doorman!"

I never visited Adrienne again in California after that visit, but we stayed in touch through letters and emails. And later on, there were phone calls that I would receive every few months into the new century to tell me and my husband that she was in town and to come meet her at the Warwick Hotel or join her for dinner at Café Loup on West 13th Street, her favorite restaurant in New York.

At the beginning of the year she died, I don't know how many people knew how close to death Adrienne already was, except, of course, for those in her immediate family. I met one of her sons for dinner that February and I told him I was concerned that I hadn't heard back from Adrienne after calling to congratulate her on a National Book Award nomination for *Tonight No Poetry Will Serve: Poems 2007-2010*. She always called back. And when she didn't that one time, I thought it was because she wanted to ignore any suggestion that she take joy in something she had made a career of not caring about. Aside from refusing the medal from Clinton, she had also only conditionally accepted her 1974 National Book Award for *Diving into the Wreck: Poems 1971-1972, stipulating that her acceptance was* on behalf of *all women*, alongside her fellow nominees Audre Lorde and Alice Walker.

Adrienne's son told me, of course, not to take the unreturned phone call personally and that his mother's long struggle with rheumatoid arthritis had curtailed her traveling and that she was living off to the side of her once very active public life. I also knew from her letters that she was suffering from a kind of macular degeneration, frontal vision loss, which was advancing slowly but irreversibly.

Of course, her leaving us all together was near, but it wasn't yet close enough to touch. And I thought, the way we always afterthink, there would have been some impromptu rite of farewell—a non-appointed moment, strange but soothing, when I could see her one last time and look into a face that I had cherished and loved for so many years. We had always been, like the truest friends, able to pick up where we left off, even with long lapses between encounters. And there were many lapses. But we lived in the same world of radical ideas and outspoken truth—life in the vernacular.

I met Adrienne Rich in the fog of a liberated, but restless and frustrating, youth. I wanted to write poetry but was already worried about how it would probably mean not having any friends. In those days, having a friend who wrote poetry meant that you didn't have the kinds of friends anybody else had. You only had weirdos and brainiacs for company. Still, it came with a kind of hot-rod spontaneity that easily and joyfully fired up my youth. I got in the habit early on of traveling with a band of misfits.

Adrienne was living then on Central Park West, and we lived six blocks down on 87th Street. Her sons (David, Pablo, and Jacob) were all at New Lincoln School and David had become one of my closest friends. Even then, having a friend whose mother was a poet was hugely impressive to both me and my brother, Kevin. And somehow (I don't remember how), we convinced Adrienne to let us come to her apartment on Saturday mornings with our friend Lauri Robertson, who also wanted to be a poet, to read poetry and explore the strains of music that poetry was making at that time.

Those meetings while growing up were the most important gatherings I would ever have. It felt as though nobody knew where we were for however-many-hours and we sat in joy on however-many-Saturday afternoons soaking up Adrienne's generosity and wit. We trusted Adrienne more than our own parents and more than we trusted the minutes in an hour. She was someone who was giving us a new way of taking in the world, how we might find a way to live in the world, with poetry, in ways beyond, way beyond, what we already knew. We were great believers in the reliable grace poetry could give us. And, I suppose, the idea that transcendence could be reliable, because that's how to describe what we were all experiencing.

In those years, Adrienne was still in a heterosexual marriage and I, of course, hadn't become the old and cynical queer person I am now. In a letter from 1988, she wrote, "We were a queer little workshop, come to think of it." And because all the poets we were reading (Merwin and Rich, James Wright, Ginsberg, et. al.) were writing poetry of resistance, I assumed that all poetry being written at that time was supposed to read like this.

Why wasn't all poetry written during this time reading like this?

I'm still asking the same that question.

As Adrienne herself wrote to the world, "*We are living in a time that needs to be lived through us.*"

The only other contemporary poems I knew back then were those last, completely startling missives written by Sylvia Plath in *Ariel*, which had, coincidentally, been published the same year, 1966, as Adrienne's own *Necessities of Life*. And perhaps it was my age, but back then I didn't read Adrienne's poems as feminist or angry or political or as written by someone who had moved away from the fixed forms of her prize-winning first book. Of course, they were all those things, at least intellectually, but what I felt then was that these were simply poems being written by someone I knew. And that revelation—knowing a woman who walked with the rest of humanity down into the subway at the corner of her block was the same person who could reach out to that much power of language—shook me. And for many years afterwards, continued to shake me—to the core of what I thought was my being.

I had no way of putting Adrienne in any literary context because I didn't have any literary context. She was my first poet, the first pilot flying me into the country of poetry. And as singular as I knew she was in a literary way, I felt lucky to have seen her plainly—which may be the reason I learned so much from her and continued to learn from her years after my boyhood crush on poetry ripened into a vocation.

At the same time I was going to Music & Art, Adrienne was teaching across the street at City College in a classroom close enough that I was able to attend her extraordinary weekly undergraduate poetry workshop. I don't think anybody knew I was a high school student. Maybe it was the facial hair. What I do know is that Adrienne didn't tell anybody. She treated me with the same respect that she had for everybody in the room. And it was in that workshop that I learned a way to talk about poetry that didn't have anything to do with how much you had read poetry. That poetry—and the way to talk about it—relied on feeling, not thinking.

The fact that over time Adrienne Rich would become one of the most truthful and luminous writers in America was something I never thought about and I considered the fact as almost ordinary—sewn into the fabric of my knowing a real artist for so many years. I never thought about her renown because it never changed who I knew she was. She always had time for her friends, and she was always an advocate for my poetry when I had no other.

I dedicated my second book of poems to Adrienne and up until the last years of her life, she always asked to see my new work, even when I was embarrassed to send it to her (especially the stuff I was writing [essays] that wasn't poetry).

From a letter, AR to MK, January 8, 2001

"Your two pieces, 'Married,' and 'A Resort of the Betrayed' made me want to read them many times. I want to urge you to edit closely and relentlessly—when the work weakens, when the energy drains, it's because you're using too many words. Go back and read Gatsby or Dickinson: Less is more. I am enclosing, should it be useful to you, the two pieces, marked-up but with admiration as well as criticism. I've put checkmarks by passages I especially like. In going through my edits please remember Pound's 'DICHTEN=CONDENSARE.' It's a pun in German: 'dicten' means to write poetry (Dichtung) but also to condense."

Of course, the greatest thing I learned from Adrienne—what I think everybody learned from her—was how to have a life in poetry, because of poetry and for poetry.

To advocate for poetry. And to stand with your dignity and your belief, however unpopular.

That there is no such thing as a career in writing, only the work that a writer is compelled to do as a response to their questioning soul, and from there outward, into the community in which the writer lives. And further still, into a world that always needs to be called out for its insistence on war and genocide. Adrienne instilled in me the idea of resisting what comes easily or what feels comfortable in my writing. She was, her whole life, a revolutionary who reinvented herself even as she endured the corporate marketing of her work.

When *Diving into the Wreck* came out (preceded by her ground-breaking *The Will to Change*), I called to ask her why both books had a photograph of a wave on their covers. "Ah, but they don't have the same cover," she said. "Look again. The wave on the new book is more threatening."

In 1999, I approached Adrienne with the idea of interviewing her for *The Paris Review*, but the list of questions they wanted me to ask her were stupid and condescending (e.g., *What time of day do you write?*). So, we told the magazine no thank you and did our own interview which we sent to the *Boston Phoenix*, where it first appeared. In that interview Adrienne spoke about where poetry was headed—which, by this time, had travelled miles away from that place of resistance, ambivalence, and ambiguity that Adrienne had taught me was where real poetry lived:

"Poetry has gotten to be very 'in,' in a way. And I've seen something I would never have imagined, which is that poetry is being com-moditized. And I thought it was uncommodifiable, because so few people really believed that it worked."

I miss my teacher as much as I miss my friend. And in trying to sort through the letters and interviews and emails to find what I want to say about her, I found this, from a letter she wrote on January 8, 2002, that turned out to be prophetic.

I'm looking straight into old age, Michael, and what I see for myself is not just aging but the effects of this lifelong debilitative disease. Hard to separate the two. I think, well, ten years from now I'll be 82, and my grandchildren, now eight, will be eighteen. What kind of life will I be capable of? Where will we all be anyway? What I care about at this point is the love of my beloveds, art, and the revolutionary idea. So this is where I'm writing poems.

Dear Michael, please let me know how you are.

Much love to you––

Adrienne.

The day after she died, I remembered something Adrienne once said that I hadn't thought about since it happened 40 years ago in 1972, when I was seventeen. Poets John Berryman and Kenneth Patchen had both died that first week of January. Berryman first, by jumping off a bridge. And then, the day after, Patchen, after years of constant pain from a spinal injury, died at home of a heart attack. I saw Adrienne at the City College bookstore after Patchen's death and the first thing she said to me was, "It's a bad week for poets."

And like that January in 1972, that last week of March 2012—a month that went out that year like a lion instead of a lamb—was just as bad a week for poets. Especially for one poet. The worst bad week for poets I have ever known. So, this would be the place from which I am writing poems.

Over Seeing

I took a picture with my eye the other day and then with my phone and I can't stop thinking about it: a man standing on the far side of a doorway in blue light—a back door on East 43rd Street, the huge space Cipriani uses for events.

It was 6:00 p.m. when I took this picture and I go back every day around the same time to see if it's still there. Which, of course it is, but I mean really *there*—within the frequency of a world that exists purely for the imagination: a blue doorway with a man standing against the door.

Is he playing a horn? Waiting for his date? Going over the reservation list?

Since I took the picture and have gone back to see it day after day, it isn't there anymore in the actual. The big brass doors that close over the doors made of glass are still there, and if you didn't know where you were, you wouldn't know the picture I took had ever existed—that there was ever this blue, and then those shadows of this blue beyond the big doors—you would never know that a man exactly like that man stood alone at a threshold so open to meaning-making.

I'm greedy and compulsive when it comes to images and I don't honor their singularity or sacredness as I should all the time. I want to be much more—what?—spiritual? than I am. Galen McKinley used to say, "anything worth doing is worth over doing" and sometimes there are days—like the first day of that blue door—when I think anything worth seeing is worth *over* seeing. I go back every day to find something that isn't there because it was there once before and because it had such an effect on me. It took me out of a world that never had a blue door in it.

But is that only a recognition of a singular beauty that anyone could see? Or is it only important because I saw it enough to put into a photograph? Of course, it was important to me, the one who took the picture of the door with its two unreadable pages of paper taped to it. And because I could see it and know it for itself and for what it radiated, I know there will be something else someday—some other version of hidden blue, something that will catch me and take my breath away.

One day, summers ago, I saw a rectangular red and white tube that was actually a kite, seemingly string-less, floating in the sky above our mystical little cottage on the beach.

There's a picture of that, too: a cloud feebly knocking against the tube, like a king at the door.

Last week, it was the back door of a restaurant in New York.

I wonder where paradise is?

There are these shining steps that lead somewhere.

Gran Torino

Even the car doesn't get a fair shake in the awful, over-the-top, idiotic and insulting Clint Eastwood movie *Gran Torino*. The car never even gets driven. And so, like everything else the camera shows us, it's as good as dead. The car's shine and perfect condition isn't even mined metaphorically. It just sits there like a glamour puss at a funeral. And the funeral that begins the movie is just a precursor to the bigger funeral the movie is—an exploration of racism that is so simplistic as to be nerve-racking. People are called racists without any explanation as to why that is so, as if merely living in a city is enough to justify the idea that, of course, racists must be living there.

Is racism too simplistic an ill to make complex? The film implies it.

And, as the racist who warms up to the kid next door, Mr. Eastwood gives his worst performance. He grunts and talks in mind-numbing monosyllables out of a script that draws, only in brief detail—along with other cutouts of characters—one lone, proverbial barber who spews racist venom even in idle conversation. Like everyone else in the movie, the barber doesn't state, he reiterates.

This is a message movie, and the message is plastered across the screen like coming attraction posters plastered along the routes for public buses. It's also a film that feels and sounds like a death rattle—as opposed to Eastman's previous films, *Mystic River* and *Bird,* which are brimming with life.

Eastwood has the energy in most of the scenes here of someone who wants either to go back to bed or just go dead because he can't shake the memory of killing someone in the war or to shake the ghost of his dead wife, who's nagging last wish was for him to get good with the church—a plot point which is clumsily personified in a pastor who is so loveless you can't help but think he'd be better off in a job where speech isn't required, perhaps funeral directing.

The film spends most of its time circling around the well-mined cliché of the jagged rhythms gang life—coming menacingly around the bend, doing mischief, coming around the bend again, and doing even more mischief, so that you know about an hour into this mess that it's all going to culminate in something horrible—which, of course, in the grand old traditional Hollywood way, it does.

The movie begins with a funeral and ends with a funeral. But unlike real life in which funerals are—even in happy families—bracketed by more living, *Gran Torino* spends its time between ceremonies justifying their purpose. We're suited more to mourn, says the movie, than we are to praise. People come together not to remember the dead as much to be reminded that they are still living, which, in itself, is this film's too blatant cry.

Isadora Duncan

Willie Mack, who ran the halfway house for drunks where I lived after going through the adjoining rehab center in Plainview, New York, told me on the day I left to go live in New York City: "Klein, just remember, you can't make things happen."

I wasn't much of a writer then, but somehow I knew that Mack's advice was bad advice for a writer. Whoever came up with the phrase *write what you know* was caught in an idea that wasn't true and, worse, just lazy thinking. Toni Morrison told her students: "Don't pay attention to that. First, because you don't know anything. And second, because I don't want to hear about your true love and your mama and your papa and your friends. Think of somebody you don't know. What about a Mexican waitress in the Rio Grande who can barely speak English? If you do end up writing an autobiography, relate to yourself as a stranger. Don't be scared to write into the unknown."

Isadora Duncan was a dancer who knew precisely where the unknown was located and then choreographed herself right into it. Her art—and there's no better place to see it happen than in the glorious performance Vanessa Redgrave gives in *The Loves of Isadora*—was of a kind that found its balance at the edge of an abyss in the somehow supernatural 1920s.

Duncan was ahead of her own politics and history in so many ways that it made her a kind of time traveler who chose modern dance so that people couldn't know what century she actually belonged to. I suppose every artist is a time traveler, in a way, being both here, but also out there, a vision that by necessity tunes into a sense of the future.

The dances made by Isadora Duncan came from her belief that she was shamelessly free, all movement arising from the solar plexus—a belief in opposition to that of the well-known jazz dancer and teacher, Luigi, who believed all movement comes from the asshole. Carl Sandburg, strangely enough (never a fan, I, of the fog whenever a cat is creeping about), wrote a line in a poem about Duncan that said: "I dance what I am." And that *I am-ness* was how Duncan thought of herself rather than calling herself a dancer—something she had been doing *before* she arrived in the body of her dancing—dancing in her mother's womb. Her mother, as it is famously rumored, dined on oysters and champagne during her pregnancy.

Isadora's artistic shamelessness included denouncing marriage, a stance she held from a young age. But she did succumb to the convention once, when she was married briefly to a Russian poet named Serge Essenin who hung himself in a hotel room in Leningrad after writing a poem in blood that ended, "There's nothing new in dying now/though living is no newer."

Isadora Duncan couldn't be bothered with the idea of economic security, giving her another kind of freedom, which helped in a conjuring of an art no one had ever seen before. Her art didn't imitate her life; it was what her life looked like. Everything that happened to her—marriage, children, politics, dancing barefoot—was manifested through her dancing. And her own way of being drew hundreds of people to watch her perform.

At the age of 19, she was the most famous dancer in the world, and her fame made her even more ethereal, more unreal, up until the end and the way of her famous death—in Nice, France, on September 14, 1927—strangled by her own scarf, when it was caught in the wheel of a handsome stranger's Amilcar CGSS automobile. She was 50 years old.

Ever since I first saw and fell in love with Isadora Duncan in *The Loves of Isadora*, she has been a role model for how to live, to write. But, in the end, I've only been able to follow her lead with an admiring heart and not a desirous one, unable to spring into the same shameless action. I don't have the life I imagined for myself as an artist, as a writer.

But there's joy after a good day of my art—some sudden daylight breaking through what can feel like a dark hour, gathering the soul-stirring idea that hasn't yet caught flight.

What is that yearning that doesn't start in language?

It will come again, as it must if it has anything to do with being alive.

Resist what I already know.

Celebrate mystery.

Dance excitingly into the unknown.

Telling My Brother's Life

In "The End of Being Known," my book about sex and friendship and the riddle of why I hadn't had an intimate relationship for 15 years, there's a part of the book that imagines my brother dying in the street—gay bashed, I guess you would call it—a dark and rhapsodic rambling based on a violence I always sensed lurked at the edge of my brother's life.

This piece of writing is near the beginning of the book to erupt it into being. And then at the end of the book, there's a sort of counterpoint to the violence, all about Andrew, the man I met online and with whom I eventually fell in love.

Both sides of that book were strokes of imagination.

And in time they both came true.

As strange as it was for love's edict to break through (Andrew, the once and seemingly everlasting elusive someone to love)—the prophesy of my brother's death was even stranger. Had I written a book of secret desires without knowing it? One awful one, one good? A love wish and a death wish? Every memoir is dangerous when it departs from actual life and enters an imagined life—when the writer forgets what must have happened and starts to follow a line of mind that personalizes the randomness of living. A memoir insists that life is most authentic when there's no turning back; when, in a dazed confession, it could all be told as if it were someone else's life.

So, that was it.

I was telling someone else's life.

I was telling my brother's life.

Every twin lives two lives—one real, one imagined—one of being alone at night and then with his twin by day; the other lit by a wondering of what life would be like without the other around. Twins co-joined are hardwired that way—born thinking what a life detached from the other life would feel like.

———

I'm the survivor. Because I thought like a survivor, even when I didn't voice it so plain.

My survivor thinking kept coming and going, both in my living and in my writing.

I'm the survivor because I can feel my brother more now than I could feel him then, in our living.

I'm the survivor because I feel survivor's guilt, not to have survived but to have always known that I would be the one to write this sentence.

I'm the survivor because we said in a game that I would survive.

I'm the survivor because my brother wanted me to be the survivor.

—

I didn't want my brother to die and I didn't secretly wish him dead, but writing about his death before it happened was—let's face it—an odd thing to do, even if it came partly out of the imagination and partly out of some innate understanding of how he survived—however shattered— in his own life.

While it was no secret to anybody who knew him that my brother was an active alcoholic and would probably die from it, he wasn't—I thought he wasn't—as close to his ending as I'd written him in my book. But that spell—what turned out to be precursor—was made even stronger because I never showed Kevin the piece of writing this spell made me write. What did I show him—what I had to show him—reading it over the phone one afternoon from an attorney's conference room—was an essay about the weird and important sexual relationship of ours when we were young, standing on the frazzled threshold of impulse and (queer?) sexual desire.

I had to read my brother the essay about this weird and important sex because it was to be published in an anthology of erotic gay memoirs, and, for it to be considered, the piece had to be cleared through the legal department of the publishing house. There's some strange stipulation whereby even if a name is changed (I changed Kevin's name to "Rex") in a piece of "non-fiction"—you still need permission from the real person in case they can identify themselves in a character.

I needed permission from my brother to tell on him.

Now that he's dead, Rex is back to being Kevin.

Writers get their people back after their people die.

People revert to the people they were.

I was very nervous on the phone when telling my brother about the anthology because I hadn't spoken to him in a long time (the silence was already there, the truth of the sex): "Um… look, I've written this piece about our incest and they want to publish it and I'm going to read it to you and ask you if it's okay because if it isn't, you can sue me or something." Kevin had to approve the "story" or it wasn't going to see the light of print. After I read it to him, I was surprised by his reaction. He very casually said, "Sure it's fine, it's a good piece, when is it coming out?"

It didn't occur to me at the time, but my brother's approval may also have been his way to not discuss the story, relieved now that the piece was written and he was away from the potential fireworks of strange sex that could have gone off too close to him. My brother may have been relieved because what I had written froze the incest in time: still painful and ambiguous, but no longer the central heating of the here and now.

When the anthology came out, Kevin called me every now and then to say that he'd seen the book in the gay section of some bookstore somewhere. (Where else would it be? The general population's interest in gay life abruptly ends at erotic memoir). But he didn't live to see my book of essays published and died never knowing I had caused his death in the middle of a summer street in the middle of a paragraph of creative non-fiction.

And now, in these many summers away from his final summer, I am thinking of the fragility of any family, once it enters that required phase of grief when we try to unravel the riddle, not of the death, but of the life. All of us die, but not all of us live.

I know that my brother died of acute alcohol poisoning, taking its last good shot at his already broken heart, but I don't know how he managed to stand in one place for so many years. Nor did I know how he lived in that one room and work in that one basement or inhabit his one mind, lubricated with fear and resentment toward most of his people, but he would occasionally break down those walls with joy, thank God—celebrating the people he knew who made—no matter how cluttered their lives—a place for art.

Like so many families into which a writer is born, I don't know if my brother ever saw me as a *practicing* artist. I was someone who wrote poems, some prose, but I was not the artist doing it, I was my brother's brother doing it. I was the big mouth with a pen who should have let lying dogs sleep in the middle of a road, a memoirist in a family made from secrets and lies.

Of the many strange unspokennesses between us, perhaps the oddest was the conversation my brother and I never had about how serious I was about my work, serious about getting it published and, finally, about finding a community of writers in a world, my world, that did not begin with writers. My brother had certainly written (though his only book of poems was published posthumously), but he was never that concerned about what would happen to his writing, a truth supported by the fact that he only sent it out on occasion.

My brother never tried to have a career, which I always admired about him, something that prevented him having the necessary ambition to grow a writing career.

Maybe he was the real artist after all.

I don't know because we never talked about it. I don't know what he thought about how real artists see themselves.

We never talked about the things I talked about with other people.

We watched movies and read books and talked about them and we watched the family go in and out on a tide we weren't riding and we talked about that.

Or we gossiped. And, like anyone who gossips, neither of us walked away from those conversations with any sense of connection, just enough news to get us to the next conversation. Enough talk to remember each other.

We didn't reveal what wasn't already in the public domain and we didn't look away when we were looking at something together.

When my brother was looking at his twin, he saw the alcoholic and the homosexual who was miraculously able to maneuver long-term relationships, which had always felt to my brother such a task of heart and mind that he spent most of his life outside of anything long-term. I can imagine him now as a painting, a picture of long-term loneliness, someone involved in the arduous task of wrangling an ocean liner to shore. And when I look at that painting and see him alone and vulnerable, under the weight of his own creation, I shudder, thinking what I have always thought about my brother and about the task of romantic love (and it's hard for me to say this without feeling smug) that what my brother saw when he was looking at me, his twin, was the fact that he couldn't have him. The sex I had with my brother was over, but I believe was still happening in Kevin's own timeline.

The twin waits for the other to stop thinking.

And because that unrequited something kept imperfecting our brotherly frequencies, we were never really there for each other when it really counted:

when my mother died and he was hospitalized soon afterwards;

when I broke up with my lover of many years and needed to get sober;

when I met Andrew and was afraid to let him meet Kevin because it was my first real relationship in 15 years and I couldn't let Andrew fall for the thing in Kevin (something softer than physical) that resembled the thing in me.

Kevin got the facts about my meeting Andrew, but my brother and I weren't in the habit of talking about our lives as they were happening. We found our language in the after-it-happened.

We found talk by rummaging around in the results.

Somehow, being born magically together activated that thing called the "virtue," being a twin and giving us the permission to not have to ask each other anything.

Of course we knew what the other was thinking. We were twins. And because we were twins, how could I not know that there would be a night like this:

he picks up the guy, which leads to the door

which leads to the stairs

which leads to an unmade bed at the center of that hot night of his hot death after that stranger leaves him alone with his heart, just before it stops.

How could I not know that my brother would be dead before I was?

—

Richard, my ex, called soon after Kevin's death to tell me—as though it were important somehow for me to know—that it felt to him as though a piece of me had died, too—not all of me, just a piece. Which piece, I wonder, but I didn't want to know, so I didn't ask. And for every twin whose twin is dead, there is the nagging—or is it misplaced?—grief, not being sure who to grieve, or which of the two had, in fact, died.

But I was sure.

Kevin was dead.

I was alive.

When I was a twin, Kevin was alive.

Doug Varone

One of the strange joys of being in love with someone is how happiness ruins everything. No more courting the dark from which—or so I believed—any meaningful writing comes. I've always worn my own darkness and haven't tried—I hope I haven't—to pretend it doesn't exist. It always feels odd to identify an experience because of how *happy* it made me feel. Except, of course, when it comes to love. But even then, even at love, I'm wary when happiness comes skipping along into my writing.

I've never understood the impulse to write out of happiness. I'm a happy person and a funny person, but I'm not a happy writer or a funny writer. I don't believe that a piece of writing has to be sad, but it does—at least for me—have to insist on acknowledging a shadow. It has to offer something that a good cop would call evidence.

The cantankerous poet/genius Alan Dugan once sat at my wobbly kitchen table in Provincetown in 1990 to offer his thoughts on my first poetry manuscript—which, as the way it is for a lot of poets, was my MFA thesis. At one point, Dugan blurted out in a spray of O'Doul's fake beer, "The dash is sentimental." Which I sort of understand, since as punctuation, it's loud. Dugan's remark reminded me of Richard Hugo's famous advice that a poem should never be sentimental but always risk sentimentality, like a ladder *almost* touching a building.

Which brings me to dance.

I wonder if dance is the one art in which we can show real joy at being alive without looking sentimental. Watching dancers dance gives me more joy than anything I know—especially a dance like Doug Varone's extraordinary *Lux*—dreamed up when Varone listened to the equally extraordinary *The Light* by Philip Glass.

I started watching dance long ago—when my own joy was more of a strategy for making poems or whatever else it was I was writing at that age, when all writing sounded and felt the same. I watched dances to look at happiness—to be reminded that happiness is, in its purest form, with the fluidity of a human body moving through space. And watching Doug

Varone's dancers reminded me there is an intelligence to the body in utter joy—a *scheme* that lets the dancer recognize the power of the body as it turns into the light and leaves the ground.

But there's gravity here, too. And what the modern dancer instinctively knows—unlike the ballet dancer who only wants to defy that pull—is that the quality of the step away from the ground feels the same as the step back to it.

*What I really wanted was some evidence
that one didn't have to lead a "literary" life …
that one could live as one pleased, and not
be shamefaced in the glare of renown (if
it ever came) at being an insurance man.*

—*James Merrill, from a* Paris Review *interview*

The Pleasures of The Cult

We're born into the cult that ends in a surname. Then there are the other family members we choose: each an island of came-to-believe. Cults, in their laser way, are the conspiratorial subtext of what a collective thinks about a certain way of living. In one such subtext, in the '70s, there was a group of us who met in the offices of a blind chiropractor named Harry Kenmore who praised, in that annoyingly self-diagnosed assignation, the Indian avatar, Maher Baba. The coolest thing about Maher Baba (aside from the fact that he sort of looked like Frank Zappa) was that, from 1925 until his death in 1969, he was silent and communicated only through the language of chalk on a blackboard, and with each powdery white stroke, he was telling the world that he'd said enough. He was telling us that it was time to live by what he said.

I had long hair then. We all did. We all wanted to look like our avatar, our savior, our One. And when I was asked to cut it for the yearly celebration in which we publicly praised his name, in the ballroom of the Barbizon Plaza Hotel, I said: never. I'd had too many of what I'd referred to as beautiful moments in my long hair. My hair had to stay long to pay tribute to the best version of my life.

In those days, in addition to the love I had for Maher Baba and Laura Nyro and the Incredible String Band, I was in love with a boy named Haydn, whose hair fell down past his shoulders and whose spirit-rhythm led us into the sunshine of our avatar in the first place. And it was probably because of Haydn, and the fact that I was following love in whatever direction it was going, that I went.

BANNED Wet Dream

One of the things I really like about Facebook—apart from the ease of maneuvering the site, gathering an extraordinary amount of useful and trivial information—is its open forum quality. Anything goes. Well, up to a point.

Josh Lehrer is a photographer who usually takes theatre photographs and portraits but one day he posted a series he called "sexy photographs" that were, I'm sure to some people, pretty shocking—not pornography, exactly, but images that were clearly the stuff of pornography: men with full erections and, in one shot in particular, a man standing with his hand on his cock in the throes of orgasm: a short milky thread captured in midair.

It's an amazing series of photographs and the bodies are pretty extraordinary, but what makes the series unique is that nothing really sexual registers on the faces of the models. Here's a tribute to people on the highway of sex where there is no traffic—in sex but not thinking about sex—no visible record of ecstasy, ambiguity, or vulnerability. The power of the pictures lies in the fact that they depict the body, without the mind, as impulsive.

They also are not pornographic because improvisation doesn't play well here. A man has come into the studio to have an erection and a photographer will take a picture of it. The man's relationship to his erection is like an appointment—over as soon the aperture opens and closes.

When I first saw the pictures, I emailed Josh and told him that Facebook was going to shut him down. And they did. But, in a funny way, seeing those pictures only that once gave them extra meaning, the way it is when you awaken from a fleeting sex dream that isn't pornographic either.

Women Who Write the World

George W. Bush can love God and his country, but goodbye to all that—I love a good conspiracy theory. I like to think most writers do because we writers are spies in this life, after all—thieves, too, who'll tell anybody and everybody who will listen what we've found.

The chain of events that culminated in the nightmare that was September 11, 2001, and its war-rallying aftermath, had more conspiracy to it than anything that had happened in America since the Kennedy assassination or—you don't even have to go back that far—Bush's presidential election, which was a conspiracy so botched that it ranked even with the O.J. Simpson trial as a travesty of American justice. In its aftermath, 9/11 provoked a national disillusionment of what we consider absolute truth.

After two planes pornographically crashed into the World Trade towers, the American public was told within 48 hours just who was responsible and which country we would be going to war with. There was hardly time to digest what really happened, and so everybody, or so it seemed, blithely went along with the revenge scenario as though we had been too long without a war, in a country that was happily summering on headlines more gossip than real news: Shark Attacks Boy in Florida; Chandra Levy Vanishes.

We were a country isolated from the rest of geography, inventing—instead of actually knowing—what was crucial about living in a world so hungry and broke. The media kept thriving by turning our loneliness into news. And then, on September 11th, they turned our shock and grief into news, too. *How could this have happened to us?* all those headlines seem say, though only to each other. How could this *not* have happened to us?

Bush had everybody believing that the so-called war on terrorism was a real war. Our national grief was so quickly manipulated to support this war—all without an actual enemy or an act of Congress to declare it. Those four hijacked planes knocked me out of the personal, and I found that I, despite being mostly an autobiographical writer, could no longer talk about myself in that way because downtown Manhattan, suddenly on fire, was the only actual subject—smaller, more concrete, more dangerous, and supernaturally close. I had become a journalist, facing a story with no tangible evidence of anything except precedent-making disaster; mentally taking notes because I was unable to devise an appropriate artistic response to this devastation.

I went numb; I went factual.

I wanted to know the facts of the world more than I wanted to feel alive in it, so tenuous was this new world.

I became a political hysteric, and I am resolutely not a political person.

I came down with BNS—Breaking News Syndrome—going against my innate distrust of the media to the point of absurdity, not getting enough of the news, scanning both the television and cyberspace for what was happening because what I had seen through a window on the 45th floor of a midtown office building somewhere around 10:00 in the morning—two hours that collapsed in apocalyptic silence—couldn't be what was actually happening. The world became a junkie, looking for a fix. And I was looking for a conspiracy angle to give the unimaginable some context, flexing my reading-the-world muscles, while my writing-the-world muscle was looking for something that could contain, and then reflect, an event of this strength.

The conspiracy angle is, of course, a fool's geometry—a tilting of truth away from what makes it true. But conspiracy is natural in the world today because it provides the ordinary citizen with a personal involvement in the impersonal (i.e., governmental predicament or cataclysmic event—shocking, political, apocalyptic-borne), something already beyond anyone's control, without having to acknowledge its uncontrollable self. Conspiracy is a way of getting involved in world policy when we are—especially intellectuals and artists—never involved in world policy. And because it is the hegemonic forces that fire up American politics, we are left in the wake and metronome-sound of policy-making rhetoric. Too much of it, and particularly under Bush, an American president who was unable to articulate an original idea—who has unbelievably been compared to Winston Churchill.

The first address Bush gave Congress after September 11th was a drum beat of war—not exactly the chamber music of statesmanship. His language of no ideas—all action without consequence—was perceived as his actually being articulate, which is dangerous for language and even more so for Americans. And when he framed his war on terrorism as a battle between good and evil, he was at his most vague. Since when has America—the largest corporate sponsor of terrorism in the world—been able to discern between good and evil?

Bush sounded, too much of the time, like someone visibly shaken, having to rise to an occasion he couldn't master, and his language was cadenced in the childish rhythm of a man who's been bullied, not influenced, by his historical time and to such a degree that he puts his country on the offense. When he was elected, his sense of the world—foreign policy, let's call it—was cloudy, at best. In his previous capacity of Texas governor, and not anything larger, Bush ordered enough deaths by electric chair to have the South black out in a violence over reason. And now, after 9/11 and later, the world is inhuman with violence.

During my search for the best language to describe this violent world, here and in Afghanistan—to cite just one geo-political landmine—I heard Sebastian Junger say something at a reading that stayed with me for weeks. He'd been reporting from Afghanistan for ABC News—an assignment unsuited to him because of his almost anti-celebrity demeanor, which, oddly enough, made his reporting that much more interesting. You listen closer to what Junger has to say because you can't quite believe he's on television.

In this particular report, Junger was talking about being holed up in a house in Kandahar with a bunch of other journalists during particularly heavy bombing, some 20 miles away. The house had been shelled weeks before by American bombs, and all of the glass in the windows had been replaced by sheets of plastic that were billowing in and out with the force of this newest bombing. In a moment of recognizing how the world had changed, Junger described the billowing plastic as "the world trying to catch its breath."

If the world was trying to catch its breath, one would only hope that America's foreign policy would be forced to lie down upon the examination table. As a nation, we are still very much acting the way we have

always acted—stomping around like an elephant, inflicting pain and suffering and calling it a fight for freedom. But freedom is a state of mind,
not a spoil of war, and somewhere along this road to oblivion, rhetoric
and real truth have blurred into a nationalistic push to to go out and
buy stuff—instructions delivered in the all-business manner of a traffic cop: Nothing to see here, move along—anything but sit down and
think about what war means and why we have to cooperate with one. An
American life, so they've been telling us, if you've really been listening, is
literally, commercially, more valuable than, say, an Afghani one.

And that one act, on a crystal-clear blue day in New York City,
was enough to rush us into defense of those valuable lives—getting this
country into a war with Afghanistan so fast and, to use a Bush-ism—with
such resolve—that any mourning over the people dead in the towers was
turned inside out before the first body was ever carried from the World
Trade Center.

Here's something from one of the more interesting conspiracy-the-
ory websites—its URL being, ominously enough, *what really happened
dot com*:

> "Sun Tsu, in The Art of War, writes that all war is based
> on deception. The people of an invading nation have to be
> deceived into thinking that they act in their own self-de-
> fense; that they are the ones to have been attacked. The
> United States government has a long history of using such
> deceptions to start wars, from claiming that the USS Maine,
> sunk by a coal-bin fire, was sunk by a Spanish mine, to
> the Gulf of Tonkin and the torpedoes that never were, to
> Operation Northwoods, in which the Joint Chiefs planned
> to stage fake terror attacks to manufacture American sup-
> port for a war against Cuba.
>
> Once a government resorts to terrorizing its own pop-
> ulation to control them, it must keep doing so, out of fear
> that a population no longer afraid will start to think clearly
> about what is going on. Terror has to become legal."

I don't know about you, but when I read something like that, I find conspiracy to be a lot more plausible than anything the government, or some forms of bandwagoning (patriotism, jingoism), can say about what's really happening. And while everybody was reassessing their relationships and whether their loves or infatuations measured up against mid-September's so violently lit reminder of the fragility of life, I was jones-ing on conspiracy. I couldn't get enough, looking through the window of conspiracy to see what Islam, terrorism, oil, Bush, and September 11th had to do with one another.

I went to hear Karen Armstrong, author of *The History of God*, speak about Islam and the whacked-out behavior of the 19 alleged terrorists on that night before their martyrdom—drinking in topless joints. "Very non-devout behavior," Armstrong said, which for her, discredited the terrorists as religious fundamentalists.

I joined an anti-war group that the playwright Eve Ensler put together and I listened to the women from RAWA—Revolutionary Association of the Women of Afghanistan—Afghani radicals who refused the burka and taught girls in their secret classrooms.

I read every conspiracy report I could find.

Those planes were actually remote controlled.

Osama bin Laden had plastic surgery two years ago.

Osama bin Laden met with an American official a few months before the attack in a hospital, over a dialysis machine.

Israel was responsible for what happened on September 11th..

Arabs and Pakistanis who worked in the World Trade Center were told to stay home on September 11th.

Conspiracy isn't the aberration of truth it's always claimed to be by the media. I think of conspiracy as an ache in the muscle—a variation seated there, but also so original that the rhetoric is overshadowed by active imagining—putting an imaginary idea behind the real thing. And instead of rhetoric—always reliable in its effect, and always a drag to sit through—conspiracy releases effervescent conjecture. There's nothing wrong with conjecture, except it's never quite dull enough to be true.

Because conspiracy is a kind of fiction, it is a driving force behind the art of fiction, and other kinds of writing. Patricia Hampl advises anyone writing a memoir to "make something up to see if it's true"—a conspiratorial idea. I think the same can be said for most writers—that they are, in a way, actively engaged in conspiracy—albeit a milder one than of the political kind. But it's a conspiracy nonetheless, something moving behind the world that we can't quite see. A writer's life is always moving in this direction.

Writers, like conspirators, state their case in a way that edges out absolute truth by holding it below what is possible. Every good writer gives us a world that we are very close to, though never completely living in. And like fiction's mission to carry us into a dream, every conspiracy theory is delivered to us from an altered state of consciousness.

A piece of writing—and none, I don't think, more persuasively than a great journalist's essay—can change your life, the way you think, or what you thought was important. One fact of writing that has become increasingly clear to me after years of reading is that many women writers have accessed this world of possibility more than their male counterparts. I don't mean to be sexist here, but revisionist.

A good woman writer isn't a biological inevitability (there are, of course, bad women writers), but, as I said, it is an aspiration to be good—one that, for me, goes past writing. I aspire to be a man who acts like a woman—not drag (I'm too hairy)—but someone who allows him/herself to go all the way through grief, valuing his vulnerability as an ecstatic moment, rather than see it as a way to avoid life. It seems to me that men have electrified history so much that it has made terrorists out of them.

I have been forced—like most of us—to listen to the voices of mostly white men my whole American life. But, thankfully, the majority of my reading has always been written by women or by men who are women. This is true especially now. Here's Jeanette Winterson, writing for *The Guardian*, excerpted from a piece called "Life on Planet Earth":

> "When are we going to take responsibility for the way we live? I can hardly believe that we are back into those '70s feminist debates about women, nature, the Earth, life, nurturing and continuity, versus men who have no respect for the natural world, and see it as they see the female body, as something imperfect, approximate and in need of a helping hand from science.

Everywhere I look, men are talking about nuclear capacity, about germ warfare, about dedicating 50 years to wipe out terrorism. The Bush administration is delighted not to have to worry about tedious environmentalists and Kyoto protocols and World Trade protesters. This is a war – and the 'big trousers' are back in charge.

I am beginning to think that the lunatics have taken over the asylum. I don't want to be genetically engineered so that I can survive war by living in a space pod. I want to live here, on Earth, the place I call home. I want it to be a safe, beautiful place to bring up children and teach them to love life and to value it. How can I do this when our leaders are treating Earth like a hotel bedroom – trash it and move on."

Not surprisingly, it is women writers who have been writing about September 11th with more grace and understanding and fierceness than anything I can find written by a man. In addition to Jeanette Winterson and Susan Sontag, who got a ridiculous amount of flak for writing the truth about American foreign policy for *The New Yorker,* prompting what was, I'm sure, her first appearance on Fox Television—the single most important piece to emerge about the events of September 11th is by Arundhati Roy, in an essay called "The Algebra of Infinite Justice":

"But who is Osama bin Laden really? Let me rephrase that. What is Osama bin Laden? He's America's family secret. He is the American president's dark doppelganger. The savage twin of all that purports to be beautiful and civilized. He has been sculpted from the spare rib of a world laid to waste by America's foreign policy: its gunboat diplomacy, its nuclear arsenal, its vulgarly stated policy of 'full-spectrum dominance,' its barbarous military interventions, its support for despotic and doctorial regimes, its merciless economic agenda that has munched through the economies of poor countries like a cloud of locusts. It's marauding multinationals who are taking over the air we breathe, the ground we stand on, the water we drink, the thoughts we think. Now that the family secret has been spilled, the twins are blurring into one another and gradually becoming interchangeable."

So, Osama bin Laden is a symptom—a bogeyman George W. Bush and Tommy Franks and Donald Rumsfeld and Condoleezza Rice and Colin Power have chased to justify a political agenda that wants, in part, to make sure oil keeps flowing into this country. Conspiratorial or not, the world fills up with our blood so that our tanks can be filled up with gas.

We drive to the mall instead of watching the government. And the government has used September 11th to support—in case you haven't been watching—the chiseling away of civil liberties, a walk away from the ABM Treaty, the detention of hundreds of people who aren't even remotely connected to September 11th, and the patent condemnation of any form of dissent. "You're either with us, or you're with the terrorists" Bush told anyone who wouldn't join his coalition against the Axis of Evil—though he was talking to Americans who didn't support a war as well.

Bush isn't the only one unwilling to consider the opposing view. The media doesn't much like it either. ABC Nightline anchor Ted Koppel introduced, during a segment on 9/11, Arundhati Roy along with cartoonist Aaron McGruder and a group of Arab students—all people in opposition to America's policy—with this warning to the audience: "Some of you may not like what we are about to broadcast. My advice to you is that you don't have to listen." Shame on him—you absolutely do have to listen.

Why in God's name wouldn't you want to listen to someone who might have a different viewpoint than your own?

What country is this?

The publishing business doesn't like opposition either. Gore Vidal's new book, *The End of Liberty*—four essays on American domestic and foreign policy—is only available in Italian and has no American publisher interest whatsoever. HarperCollins declined to release Michael Moore's book, *Stupid White Men and Other Excuses for the State of the Nation*, because, it said, "it's a matter of publishing a book about the world situation when the world situation has changed."

Thank God people are writing in opposition, are resisting. The hope is that more people keep writing dangerous books and avoid trade houses altogether. Go to the small presses instead, where the corporate view of success doesn't hold. Big American business is the real culprit in the mess that is geo-politics, and has ensured that the world is, now—now that we, a super-power, have been attacked—officially dangerous.

The real danger here is the horrifying decision of who eats and who starves. The war on terrorism is, in effect, a strategy to make sure the satiated still rule over the dispossessed. Instead of using September 11th as a bridge of understanding to a world Americans don't know or care much about, we are making sure we drop enough bombs this time to destroy the bridge for good.

How does one respond to the world now? The broken open world?

How does one respond as an artist, as a human being?

You have a vision. You resist. This combination makes you a visionary.

A fourth grader in Houston, Texas named Carmen Penny wrote about the war in Afghanistan this way:

> "If you're lucky in this life, a window
> appears on a battlefield
> between two armies. And when the
> soldiers look into the window
> they don't see their enemies, they see
> themselves as children
> and they stop fighting and go home
> and go to sleep.
> When they wake up, the land is well again."

That poem had me writing poems again.

During the first weekend after September 11th, I went to Holy Cross Monastery in West Park, New York, where poems came to me after a two-year reprieve. Something, obviously, about the world had brought the music back into the room. Prose felt too factual now, too unable to capture the feelings I had about politics, survival, and conspiracy. I couldn't get turned on by a paragraph as much as I could by the risk of going out on a limb of one poetic line. The great Russian poet Vladimir Mayakovsky wrote: "The line is a fuse." And I could feel that idea in my blood.

I wanted to write poems that talked about September 11th without telling the story of September 11th, which was a way of me being a woman writer—igniting the psyche with associational, rather than with historical, relevance. That story of September was already so surreal, so authentic, it didn't need anything more from an artist, a writer—an act of terrorism that may have been, as composer Kalheinz Stockhausen said, getting hell for it, "the greatest work of art that is possible in the whole cosmos."

The story had been told by 19 violent men who couldn't remember being women, or children, or whether their religion said it was okay to get drunk or laid. But they were also men who, in their act of desperation, made a visionary out of the poet Carmen Penny—a girl who will someday be a woman.

When that happens, let's turn what's left of the world over to her and to others of her kind.

How Some People Happened

Steve Jobs designed every Apple product to fall asleep so he wouldn't have to turn it off. He was afraid to die.

Willi Smith was a hugely successful African American fashion designer who made clothes that were big enough to swim in—his signature style. Anybody who wore something designed by Willi Smith was making a statement about being hidden. This was the fashion in the '70s.

The reason Willi Smith made clothes so big was because he was sexually abused as a child. Willi Smith came into his artistic being by reaching back to his trauma and retrieving the thing that could have prevented it. If the perpetrator couldn't see him, how could the perpetrator touch him?

Willi Smith made clothes people got lost in because Willi Smith got lost in his own people and didn't know where his body was living, inside his own clothing, or where his body stopped and another body began.

Stephen Sondheim lived next door to Katharine Hepburn, who complained about the racket he was making on his grand piano—the music which became the show, *Company*. To appease Hepburn, Sondheim switched over to electric piano, which is why the score for *Company* sounds so different than the other scores Sondheim wrote. It's brassy because he took the grand piano out of it.

This next one may be wrong because, like most of my thinking, I can't remember how I know it—but Gaudi's Roman Catholic Sagrada Familia church came to its eventual design only after the architect took his first model for the building and turned it upside down.

The design building on the campus of Goddard College looks the way it does because it was built from the ground up, without any architectural plan whatsoever (how does it stay up?).

A bowler hat is rolling through the woods. That's all they had at first. But the Coen Brothers knew there had to be a bowler hat rolling through the woods, so they made a film called *Miller's Crossing* to figure out who was wearing that hat and how it got into the woods. They moved out from that central image and wrote the screenplay.

From an interview with an inmate on death row, San Quentin, which took place on the night before he was to be executed.

Q: *What are you going to miss?*

A: *Coltrane.*

When Maya Angelou was seven years old, she was raped by her mother's boyfriend, who was then shot to death by a group of family members. Instead of feeling relief or that that his killing could somehow balm her trauma, Angelou became more traumatized, feeling responsible for killing the man who raped her. And because she had told somebody how she was raped, she thought her voice had the power to kill. Maya Angelou stopped talking for 20 years. Then she wrote, *I Know Why the Caged Bird Sings.*

The artificial leg that the Bible salesman swipes in Flannery O'Conner's "Good Country People" means nothing until—at the story's climax—the entirety of the leg's meaning has accumulated.

Beverly Bentley, once married to Norman Mailer and the mother of his children, once dated Miles Davis—which, according to Beverly, who told me this story, was more than a casual fling. When books about Miles Davis's life were published, Beverly skimmed them all to see if she was mentioned, and when she couldn't find anything about their relationship, she called Davis and asked why.

"Because you're white," he said.

Louise Gluck

Louise once told me during a conversation we had after giving a reading the library in Montpelier, Vermont that all the poems she wrote that were to be published in her book, *The Wild Iris*, came to her one summer as is and were barely revised.

She said that was the summer when the last thing she wanted to do was write poems. She said that was the summer she wanted to make a meal or take a walk, or do laundry even, than write a poem.

She said she wrote the poems that became *The Wild Iris* so that they would leave her alone and she could get back to her everyday routine, which definitively did not include writing poems.

The "I" at the End of the World

I've been thinking about the end of the world for as long as I've been in it. It was my primary childhood fear—a projection, a therapist would probably tell you—of my off-kilter family life. And the end was going to come because China and Russia were enemies of America and eventually one of them was going to drop a nuclear bomb on New York City, where I lived on 12th Street. And it would all happen without warning, in the middle of a Saturday afternoon. Thank God for the movies my mother took me to—even if they were way too provocative (*Who's Afraid of Virginia Woolf?*, *The Pumpkin Eater*). The parallel realities in these movies gave me hope about the future. Maybe, I thought, we do survive.

I've moved only slightly away from this fear I invented in childhood. Most of my nuclear family is dead. And there are days—end of summer days, especially—when I forget about the end of the world completely, even as it teeters on its axis more hazardously than before. The world—I've concluded—is simply a machine that will eventually career from two opposite bad habits into collision: neglect and overuse. Like the beings that inhabit it, hasn't the earth always been in some phase of departure?

We all know this. But there are poets who draw on this knowing for inspiration.

Dana Levin and Laura Kasischke (among others) contributed poems as part of a feature the *New York Times* published long ago called—with a cloying kind of aw-shucks sentimentality—"It's the End of the World," as triggered by the infamous Mayan calendar prediction about the end to civilization. Generic as it was—in an effort, I suppose, to lighten the message—the title couldn't diffuse the seriousness of the poetry that followed.

"Morning News" by Dana Levin ends like this:

> The death of ice, of food, of space, what
> we call Doom —
>   which might be a bending —

a flow of permissions —

to forge a mutant form —

Time is almost always ambiguous in a poem that lasts across time—nonlinear, cosmically (or comically) stacked, ordered like a dream. And the central idea in "Morning News" is that the end is the beginning of something else, or—more trenchantly—somewhere else. Or, that the world's ending is not quite finished with imagining how to keep it intact, eulogized in the concluding lines of another Levin poem, "At the End of My Hours."

> I couldn't quite
> quit some ideas — trees and chocolate.
> I couldn't stop yammering.
> over the devastated earth
> pining for nachos — prescription drugs
> and a hint of spring, though I could see
> the new desert — its bumper-crop
> of bone and brick
> from shipwrecked cities — where now
> the sons and daughters of someone tough
> are on the hunt for rat — the scent of meat
> however mean and a root
> sending an antenna up, to consider
> greening — what poems built their houses for
> once, in a blindered age, teaching us
> the forms we felt, in rescue — hoarded-up scraps
> whirling around my cave
> trying to conjure peaches

The poem staggers along like the charting of a fever dream—the way the bedraggled father and son stagger along in Cormac McCarthy's *The Road*—through the end of a world that's collapsed, even though Levin's future-speaker isn't ready to quit just yet (or is she just crazy?). She's held to the idea of living because she still has the capacity to remember.

This haunting displacement (or is it stubbornness?) informs a very different poem about endings, Rilke's "Requiem for a Friend" (I'm thinking of the Stephen Mitchell translation), in which a woman's recent death is nuanced by her ghostly return, which feels, to the poet, way too early:

> I have my dead, and I have let them go,
> and was amazed to see them so contented,
> so soon at home in being dead, so cheerful,
> so unlike their reputation. Only you
> return; brush past me, loiter, try to knock
> against something, so that the sound reveals
> your presence ...

As it is in many Rilke poems of spiritual restlessness (the world stops and eventually begins again, but changed), Levin's "Morning News" ends on a turn and invents a place without the inconvenience of human beings or, at the very least, advocates for a different kind of being: forged, mutant.

The mutant is made by the world advancing, splitting off, or devolving. Or the mutant enters the world as something from beyond our atmosphere. I'm thinking of the movies (*Invaders from Mars* and even, in its way, *Invasion of the Body Snatchers*) where the stranger comes to town (in a spaceship, as it so happens) to signify the end of the world— particularly since these movies were all made in the '50s, the height of America's atomic testing program. The interplanetary messenger is always bringing to Earth some version of doomsday with him.

By now we've been living with the end of the world as a subject so long that it *not* happening might be more mythic. "The nuclear age produced a nuclear consciousness and nuclear psyche, but not a nuclear imagination," wrote Steve Erickson in an essay called "The Apocalypse—Stay Tuned." But it is also with this particular imagination that is responsible for catastrophe—the trope of choice in the American disaster movie. If you can't visualize the end, it's not coming. This gives poets the freedom to look at apocalypse as a gateway to a language that describes something even bigger: the threat of an empty universe in which the real subject is silence.

How does a poet write their way into such inevitability without resisting it? Or is the poem that faces the world in its conclusion just an open invitation to make something complicated read as simplistic? (Think of the overly obvious poems written after 9/11 that couldn't get out of the way of four airplanes and two towers collapsing). Jim Schley's seminal anthology, *Writing in a Nuclear Age*, published originally as a special issue of the *New England Review* and *Bread Loaf Quarterly* in 1983, consisted of prose and poetry that dealt with the idea of nuclear extinction before those longer eves of destruction—terrorism and climate change—had revealed themselves in our theater of interpretation. Some of the work in the book is naive and unimaginative; some of it is appropriately haunting.

"When," by Sharon Olds, couples nuclear anxiety with a kind of suburban malaise.

> I wonder now, only when it will happen,
> when the young mother will hear the
> noise like somebody's pressure cooker
> down the block, going off. She'll go out in the yard,
> holding her small daughter in her arms,
> and there, above the line of the trees,
> she will see it rising, lifting up
> over our horizon, the upper rim of the
> gold ball, large as a giant
> planet starting to lift up over ours.
> She will stand there in the yard holding her daughter
> looking at it rise and glow and blossom and rise,
> and the child will open her arms to it,
> it will look so beautiful.

Instead of driving predictable panic through a scene of predictable panic, Olds takes the poem in another direction. Awe and surrender end the stanza, but these impulses are also implied by the indelible and chilling opening declaration: "I wonder now only when it will happen." It's not only the world that ends, but a kind of thinking about the world, too.

William Stafford's "Next Time" uses the threat of extinction to talk about the quality of attention when it is lifted by future-hope.

Next time what I'd do is look at
the earth before saying anything. I'd stop
just before going into a house
and be an emperor for a minute
and listen better to the wind
or to the air being still.
When anyone talked to me, whether
blame or praise or just passing time,
I'd watch the face, how the mouth
has to work, and see any strain, any
sign of what lifted the voice.
And for all, I'd know more—the earth
bracing itself and soaring, the air
forest and water, and for every person
the body glowing inside the clothes
like a light.

If writing the nuclear threat has been eclipsed by a now-slow-er-moving catastrophe, it's an important difference, considering the end of the world is something that reconfigures the language we use to talk about it. The end will probably be up to the world itself, not decided by a button on a control panel behind the curtain at some Cold War secret Oz location—how I used to imagine when I was masterminding my own childhood fear.

The function of the "I" in a poem of apocalypse written now pulls further and further from the ego and, in many instances, the political. The "I" in the Olds poem has grown into one who sees beyond a merely radioactive horizon—thus underscoring a curious change in perspective: the end of the world as a philosophy about the end of the world. Which is lucky for poetry. Nothing is literal until it actually happens.

End of Days—the slogan, the commodity, the live wire sending its current through the hand of the poet writing about it—has, of course, become unavoidable as we draw closer to it. Levin suggests that we are already at the end of something—if not the world, at least our thinking around the idea that the world never ends.

Other poets (all women) have let the end of time influence—even if fleetingly—their ethos: Claudia Rankin, *Don't Let Me Be Lonely*; Laura Kasischke, *Space in Chains*; Adrienne Rich, *Tonight No Poetry Will Serve*; Chase Twitchell, *The Ghost of Eden;* Louise Gluck, *A Village Life*; Jorie Graham, *Place*; and two books published in 2013, Christina Davis, *An Ethic,* and *The Cloud That Contained the Lightning* by Cynthia Lowen, a book of poems that speaks through the voice of J. Robert Oppenheimer, "father of the atom bomb," the book's conflicted narrator.

These books are all extraordinary, and I would also include on that list a man—although he may not be an obvious choice—Jack Gilbert and his book, *The Great Fires.*

When he died in November of 2012, Gilbert interrupted the books I was then reading because I had to stop and go back to his work (you always want to hear someone's voice immediately after they die to be certain the world didn't take what they sounded like) and to the poems before *The Great Fires* for a sense of the whole life he gave us, writing in the voice of a man surviving: a dramatic whisper, sounding, Look! Here's what's left. The end of the world in a Gilbert poem is a subject that enlarges the "I" into a witness of a personal experience, though also of the world experiencing itself. Here is the conclusion of what may be Gilbert's signature poem, his core belief, "A Brief for the Defense."

> "...There is laughter
> every day in the terrible streets of Calcutta,
> and the women laugh in the cages of Bombay.
> If we deny our happiness, resist our satisfaction,
> we lessen the importance of their deprivation.
> We must risk delight. We can do without pleasure,
> but not delight. Not enjoyment. We must have
> the stubbornness to accept our gladness in the ruthless
> furnace of this world. To make injustice the only
> measure of our attention is to praise the Devil.
> If the locomotive of the Lord runs us down,
> we should give thanks that the end had magnitude.
> We must admit there will be music despite everything.
> We stand at the prow again of a small ship
> anchored late at night in the tiny port

looking over to the sleeping island: the waterfront
is three shuttered cafés and one naked light burning.
To hear the faint sound of oars in the silence as a rowboat
comes slowly out and then goes back is truly worth
all the years of sorrow that are to come."

We must risk delight, the poem instructs us and live to an end with magnitude; to take on happiness, in spite of the world trying to eat our happiness. To fight for it; to know that it isn't only possible, but a necessity of life. We must have the stubbornness to accept our gladness in the "ruthless/furnace of this world." The poem makes joy even larger and an essential human condition by framing it with dread. "There is laughter/ every day in the terrible streets of Calcutta."

Jack Gilbert's poems are complex and spiritually audacious. He is among a rare breed of writers who see the world as a love object (Nazim Hikmet and Seamus Heaney are like this, too) while still writing with the sharpness of its blade, which makes the poems bigger in the mind than they appear on the page. (The poems in *The Great Fires* are never longer than one stanza). And because, even in their measured gestures of longing, they are also poems willing to be overtaken by the world's stark and sometimes sudden outbreaks of beauty, they feel written to be read as one long footnote, referring to Hokusai's iconic woodblock print, "The Great Wave off Kanagawa." Something formidable is about to hit the shore but is caught, suspended, in the last phase of its catastrophe.

Perhaps, like Dana Levin, and all the other singers underground, Jack Gilbert considered the end of the world his muse, not the disaster popular culture would have us believe—an invitation for his mind to go inside his lyric without sounding the alarm. To go inside that lyric takes a kind of psychic will that can intuit the edge of the abyss—the what-is-ness that gives a poem about the end of the world its sense of liberation.

Writing in the Nuclear Age was my first exposure to a poetry of danger, understanding that Armageddon was something poets have been thinking about a long time. I think that subject has taken on a lexicon today that is more elliptical and unsettling than it was in the poems Schley included in his anthology.

The new writing about the end of the world (or is it *for* the end of the world?) may simply be an extension of our outrage against corporate greed and various forms of biotechnology—the way, in my childhood, I looked to the nuclear threat as a more workable explanation for why my household felt so threatening.

Childhood is the laboratory for making meaning and my sense of meaning was helped by absorbing the images I saw on television, all those old science fiction invasion movies. The alien metaphor wasn't lost on me because I, too, felt like a stranger in a strange land. I'm in my last act, and I've gone from watching space invaders, body snatchers, and radioactive insects to becoming obsessed, like other Americans, with the vampire and the shapeshifter. And, just last week, the resurrected, as they are depicted in the French thriller series *The Returned*—about a group of dead villagers who return to the land of the living years later and try to resume their lives with as little bother as possible after devastating their idyllic mountain community with their reappearance.

What's different about these villagers who've returned is they have none of the usual signs (insatiable hunger, bad skin) of a zombie's life. And, even more crucial, they're not certain they're dead until somebody tells them. In other words, they all look and sound like you and me, with the end of the world the farthest thing from their minds, since it ended already. Sort of. Life after life is their version of the rapture.

But being dead is not the same thing as being erased. And what the poets are telling me—some of them, and many of those I love—is that the dilemma of being alive at the beginning of the twenty-first century (after taking into account the unending casualties of war) is that I might not get to have my own death; "we were young we knew how to die/but not how to last," Mark Conway says at the hinge of his poem, "in the ruins." And I think in that lowercase, nonpunctuated statement, the poet identifies the essential question of our time: how do we live in a world racing faster to its own death than we are?

My copy of *Writing in a Nuclear Age* is thirty years old. I wonder why I've kept it all these years. It's a good book, but not a great book, and it started falling apart a few months ago. Maybe I keep it so I can look at the haunting photograph on the cover—from *FIRE*, a play by Peter Schumann's Bread and Puppet Theater. I dropped the book the other day and all the pages came loose and scattered to the floor. And as I was putting the pages back in, I knew they were out of order, which—I was magically thinking—perhaps made the poems lose the danger that was there when they first were written.

Looking Into A Poem

A fiction writer once told me that she believed most American poetry was apolitical and self-centered. Here's the poem she wrote to support that idea:

> I was looking out the window
> upon a field
> thinking about myself.

I can see her point proven in the poem she wrote to prove her point. In the poem, as soon as the narrator enters, s/he wipes away any idea the poem might have had to continue with the field.

I don't think all American poetry reads this way, but there is a lot of it that does.

There are poets who make themselves sound like any person in a poem—a somebody who just happened to come along; a somebody the poem is for. And in that way, the *I* also becomes the *you*.

Some poets get out of the way of the poem and are concerned with what is there, what is occurring, not necessarily what they think about what is there. Elizabeth Bishop was like that.

Or does thinking and looking happen in the same eye, through recognition?

Gerald Stern sees and works like that.

Gerald Stern said some great things in an interview on the *Rumpus* website once—that some of the poets in the edition of *The Best American Poetry* the year he was included wrote endlessly about nothing; they were narcissistic, with no cogent subject matter.

Gerald Stern said: "We're destroying the earth! We live in a country that's governed by confusion and lies and that operates through greed and selfishness and cruelty. We've killed or forced into exile two million Iraqis. Where is the poetry? What are our important poets doing?"

In 1989, at a publication party for a book I can't remember, I asked John Ashbery if he would contribute a poem to an anthology I was making about the AIDS crisis. Ashbery said: "I'm sorry, my poems don't have subject matter."

If real poetry rises only out of fragments, then the narrative impulse could be taken as narcissistic, as it keeps insisting on a longer line, which gives more space for the self to enter. The more self that enters the poem, the more like prose a poem can become.

The difference is the line and the way the mind breaks over the line and the way the line breaks over the mind.

If the poetic line is a kind of fragment, poems at their most essential happen with an understanding of how those fragments lean into what consciousness sounds like.

As soon as the poem reaches for more narrative, the hand of the writer falls more heavily on the line becoming longer than if that same hand wrote a line that was shorter.

Those few who have [a] nuclear imagination not only confront the abyss but are liberated by it.

　　—*Steve Erickson*

Calvin the Great

It was an exciting Derby in 2009 because a long shot, Mine That Bird (50-1), won the race, having arrived at Churchill Downs in true Cinderella fashion—in a trailer pulled by a pick-up truck driven by a horse trainer who was on crutches after having suffered a broken leg. And while the horse, of course, is a champ, the story here is also about the jockey, Calvin Borel.

Borel won the Kentucky Derby two years in a row, and with the same strategy for both wins—finding an opening and then shimmying his charge along the inside rail to the finish line. Also, his after-race patter to the pony girl was completely uncharacteristic of most jockeys I know (and I've known a few) who've won that race. Borel was obviously thrilled.

I don't know how many Derbies you've seen live or on television, but most of the riders are too tired, too inarticulate, or just too laid back to give you a sense that what they accomplished was, for one thing, death defying (never mind that they just made a lot of money for the owner and the trainer).

Calvin Borel carried on like a drunk at the after party—screaming and high-fiving every racetrack denizen who passed him as grandly he steered Mine That Bird into the winner's circle. He was so ecstatic with his accomplishment and so completely in love with the horse he was sitting on that the spectacle was, to my mind, the first authentic reaction to the dizzying reality of this kind of victory. *Of course, I'm thrilled* every nerve in his jockey body was saying. And suddenly, all the jockey reactions from the past seemed robotic by comparison.

Staring deeper into the sport, I now see the truth about all of us living in an age in which real joy isn't about contentment anymore since life, lately, has gotten really dark. All Calvin Borel was thinking about, I'm sure, was how he made the inside rail of a racetrack his God a *second* time. For me, watching his victory, and remembering the newest tenant in the White House, and how everyone has been looking for a long time at money and war and nuclear power, I felt that this horse, the way he got here, as he did, all the way from New Mexico, the 50-1 and his jockey's enthusiasm—all of it—is emblematic of our new way of living in America: an uncharacteristic presence of something actually becoming true.

Mary Ruefle

I knew Mary Ruefle was a poet before I read a single line she'd ever written. I think we all knew. This was Bennington College, 1970-something—spring, it probably was. Mary and I were both undergraduates (she was ahead of me by a year or two) and part of a group of like minds who loved poetry but who were mostly too busy—some of us—with more earthly concerns, like getting laid or figuring out if we were bisexual or full-blown queer. Mary, it seemed to me, had a shameless way of being in the world best exemplified by the fact that she said things nobody else even thought about. "You've lengthened," she once exclaimed, upon seeing me again after a school break.

Of course, Mary had—though nobody would have known what to call it then—a literary presence, meaning she was serious in a way that went beyond thinking like a college student—the way I remember a lot of us were put in the awkward position knowing we might be artists but only if we were willing to learn more than we already knew.

In truth, I didn't know Mary Ruefle well, though I wanted her attention. It feels, in memory, like I was a little too intimidated by her to ever really know her. But also, I didn't know her well because, even at a place like Bennington (with only around 400 full-time students in those days), there were circles of people that never intersected. I admired Mary because of her poetry, because she wanted to do something so few people could do and because she was something special in an already special place. And even if I didn't know my own heart as a poet or writer, I certainly could see it in her, which gave me pleasure and hope—the way her *Selected Poems* has done for me all these many years.

Though that book was something of an event when it was published, Wave Books wrapped it the way Wave Books likes to wrap all of their books: in a generic eggshell-colored cover, only providing the title and its author. Also, the publisher decided to run the poems from an assortment of Ruefle's previous books all together instead of breaking them up according to publication history (though they are still arranged chronologically).

The order gives a sense—or rather, adds to the sense—of the cumulative force in Mary's work—meaning that whenever I read one of the poems, the narrative and the images gather more and more insight as they fall to the bottom of the page. The poems sparkle with life, never standing still for too long. Many of them are written in an idiosyncratic, mysterious voice, sly, very funny, ambiguous, and, at times, surprisingly pious.

The structure of a Ruefle poem varies but settles often into a single stanza of varying length, giving the impression that everything in the poem is happening at the same time. As such, it feels as if it can be held that way in the psyche. *We live in the mind*, Wallace Stevens said—an idea Ruefle epitomizes in an exquisite stretch across art and geography in "The Intended":

> One wants so many things …
> One wants simply, said the lady,
> to sit on the bank and throw stones
> while another wishes he were standing
> in the Victoria and Albert Museum
> looking at Hiroshige's Waterfall:
> one would be able to paint
> like that, and Hiroshige wishes
> he could create himself out of the
> Yuro sea spray in Mino province where
> a girl under the Yuro waterfall wants
> to die, not quite sure who her person is,
> but that the water falls like a sheet of tin
> and another day's thrown in the sieve;
> one can barely see the cherry blossoms
> pinned up in little buns like the white hair
> of an old woman who was intended for this hour,
> the hour intended to sit simply on the bank
> at the end of a long life, throwing stones,
> each one hitting the water with the *tick* of
> a hairpin falling in front of a mirror.

Desire and painting, dying too soon, time examined, time slowed down, and then that extraordinary moment at the end: cinematic evidence of "this hour" and its emotional meaning to locate the thing—shocking, almost—which supports it. The poem ends with an emblem of order, of order relinquished—a hairpin falling—and the word *tick*: falling into italics to give it its sound. So delicate it becomes, in a beat, momentous.

In her poem "Replica," Ruefle paints another scene around being here by not being here that reaches back, in part, to Keats and his negative capability: that transcendent impulse to live in the uncertainty or mystery of being human without resorting to explanation—an act of faith, but with more of the occult in it. Here's the beginning of that poem:

> You've wasted another evening
> sitting with imaginary friends,
> discussing the simplest possible
> arrangement of an iris.
> The sky, too, like a delicate dress
> streaked with beach, has been thrown away.
> Once you wanted to be someone else
> or another thing altogether: an iris in April,
> or its pistil, just that, a prayer so small
> it was only rumored. What can it matter?
> You know now your own life doesn't belong to you,
> the way a child defects into his childhood
> to discover it isn't his after all.

There are two Rilkean echoes here, which recall his sense of requiem: "Once you wanted to be someone else" and "[...] into his childhood/to discover it isn't his after all." There's a variation on a James Wright variation on a line by Rilke, too: "You've wasted another evening" (Rilke's famous "you must change your life" which James Wright turned into "I have wasted my life"). Everything that happens in "Replica" is an act of an undeterred imagination, and if one were to track the ideas in these poems, one would still not be able to arrive at a single motif—too many things are going on.

As soon as you've landed somewhere in a poem, Ruefle is already starting mischief somewhere else. When Dickinson famously suggested *tell it slant*, she was instructing us to look somewhere else, and Ruefle is always looking somewhere else. What makes her so unusual compared with her contemporaries is how the central power of the poems comes out of an encounter triggered by poetic tension and not so much by any *a-ha!* moment that generally accompanies, *what I want to say is …*

—

In Ruefle's "My Emily Dickinson"—an essay from her remarkable and innovative book of lectures, *Madness, Rack and Honey*—a competitive tug, perhaps, against Susan Howe's book of the same title—Ruefle calls on Dickinson as someone who "possessed Language, and because of it—not for it, but because of it—she died and did not simply decease." Possessing language and being possessed by language is the revelation that governs many of the poems here. The poet keeps taking her language as far out on the bridge of faith as it will go, even to somewhere resembling an afterlife:

> I lived like a god.
> My thin back walking out the door,
> my heart of mayonnaise.
>
> I put halos on heads
> and they cursed me.
> Even the posh deserve names.

("Proscenium Arch")

This is not the first mention of God in the *Selected Poems*. There is, in fact, a kind of religion (that arises in the work, as evidenced in the poems "A Picture of Christ." "Heaven on Earth," "Mercy," and "The Beginnings of Idleness in Assisi"). Would it be fair, then, to surmise that Ruefle probably read the Bible as a supreme fiction, even if, for a poet as innovative and iconoclastic as she is, Ruefle can still have a reverence for the world that is surprisingly devout:

Here and there, between trees,
Cows lie down in the forest
In the midafternoon
As though sleep were an idea
for which they were willing
to die.

("Barbarians")

Death and its ebbing currents among the living is a vital subject for Ruefle—particularly in "The Passing of Time," which parcels out the almost flat language of grief to more accurately put forth what grief looks like in a scene of domesticity:

My mother has been dead six months
when my father remembers, as if for
the first time, that she is dead
and pads out across his deck
to lower the flag to half-mast.
Seeing that it already hangs midway
on the pole (snapping at the wind,
collapsed in damp heat, as if it were
her hair) he is startled and asks
Who died? I say Mother and after a while
he says Ah! Then let it fly a little longer.

The "pads out" jumps away (and lands perfectly) from the narrative. But the poem is still made of one clear tone, with the straight-ahead-ness of a story that only tells us what happens, with nothing more ornate than a flag adorning it. And we get two surprises here: the parenthetical "snapping at the wind,/collapsed in damp heat, as if it were/her hair," and Ruefle (or somebody borrowing her "I") in the room at the end (here in the land of the living), where the "I" suddenly materializes, like Joseph Cotton as Jedediah Leland in *Citizen Kane,* rolling his wheelchair out of the shadows and into the sunlight. "Who died? I say Mother and after a while/he says Ah!" is a revelation not only for the father, but for us, too, because the question is answered the way it is at the theater, in real time.

—

There's a YouTube video of Mary reading in Berkeley where she says she feels honored to be in the city of ideas, that she's never been to the city of ideas, that she hopes she has written something suitable. But Ruefle is the Poet Laureate of the City of Ideas—surreal and lyrical and deeply moving all at the same time. Perhaps, in some private joke of hers, Ruefle was saying she felt redundant in that place, and couldn't differentiate where or who she was. But she is also, in the end, a maker of fables—a fabulist. And I mean that as high praise if fable refers to the literary form that includes almost everything you can think of—animals (real and imagined), the natural world, everything you've ever read, magic, found objects—turning them into something connected enough to thrive in one stanza. Mary's fables generally begin with both a real thesis and an imagined one:

> Late that night it rained so hard the world
> Seemed flattened for good.
> But the grocer knew the earth had a big gut
> and could hold more than enough.
> ("The Tragic Drama of Joy")
> Or:
> This is the story of why my shoes
> lie in a row at the bottom of my closet.
> In the state of Virginia, on the North American
> continent, there was a wasp.

> ("The Edge")

I can hear Wallace Stevens here with his "I placed a jar in Tennessee,/ And round it was upon a hill ..." It's the consciousness of the poem itself that a Mary Ruefle poem defends, and is her higher calling, more than, say, any technical skill she exercises to bring her subject into focus. This is why the poems are almost immediately recognizable, not only as something she has written (as with any great poet, nobody sounds like her), but as one out of which she has written *herself,* this through the use of the "I"—particularly when that "I" begins the poem.

The "I" is almost always bigger than the mere self and is not completely reliable. Consider the following first lines: "I walk into the restaurant, a genetic legacy" ("Tilapia"); "I'm sorry to say it but fucking/ is nothing [...]" ("Merengue"); "I laid my happiness in a field" ("My Happiness"). Or the obvious "I was born in a hospital. I stank." ("Nice Hands") or probably not true: "I was a failure as a gingerbread maker" ("Critique of Little Errors").

Mary Ruefle is also one of the only living poets I know who makes magical thinking a strategy in the making of poems (Lynn Emanuel— another Bennington graduate—does this too to a degree). Her intelligence and playfulness engage with a shared reality, but she also thinks hard enough about something out of that shared range until it's true. The poems aren't slight or in any way occasional, even when they appear so because of their strong documentary feel and a dialectic she stands on its head: her argument is with the argument. Here's the end of a poem called "The Cart":

> The world might be in agony, but I don't think so.
> Somewhere a woman is swathed in black veils
> and smiling too. It might be the eve of her baptism,
> the day after her son hit a pole.
> How can she signal her acceptance of life?
> What if a hummingbird enters her mouth? I hate
> the thought, whizzing by in red clothes.
> Yet I admire its gloves. Hands are unbearably beautiful.
> They hold on to things. They let things go.

Like many of her poems, "The Cart" reads like a spell in a fable, and like a prayer, too. Ruefle embraces both negative capability and duende. The knowledge that poems hold the meaning of both living and dying at the same time.

In her introduction to *Madness, Rack and Honey*, Ruefle writes: "I am a writer and writing is my natural act, more natural than speaking." In the same Berkeley YouTube video I mention above, she says, during a rare moment of looking up from the poems, "I apologize for not having much to say about these poems. They're all based on things that happened to me." Okay, but I also like to think the apology is a kind of joke she is telling herself. Everybody knows that even after everything that happens to us, we still live in the mind.

The Glass Menagerie

(A.R.T., Cambridge, 2013)

The character Laura, played by Celia Keenan-Bolger, makes her first appearance on stage by crawling out of a couch. It is a genius move. And something happens to the character, Amanda, played by Cherry Jones when she changes into that dress. She travels.

She stands in for the idea of a future husband seen through a curtain of jonquils.

She is dying of loneliness, like everyone else.

Her dress with its original flowers all missing will last as long as reality's next great upheaval—the next time she calls to Tom, her son, who will make his departure before she returns to her present, where ghosts inhabit time before they find the bodies to make them recognizable to other people. Even the gentleman caller, who we believe from the moment a theatrical breeze follows him up the stairs, will take over the whole production, with Laura in it. More than anybody else in this memory play, Tom is banking on a dream to cure him of the '30s.

Marie Howe

I don't know where to begin trying to talk about Marie Howe. She has been—for more than 30 years—a close friend, a sister-confident, and always the remarkable poet and thinker that people know her to be. I can't think of a conversation I've had with Marie in which she didn't say something that surprised me. I've been lucky in life that way—grateful to be among friends who are always surprising each other with some insight, or something funny, or with a look followed by a description of something that wasn't previously there.

This is a conversation we had in 2020:

MK: What inspires you lately?

MH: There's a guy in Washington Square Park who's made a puppet called Sticks. The puppet is a homeless guy—vitally alive. He's a drinker and a dancer. Whenever I go to the park, we look around for Sticks. And when we're lucky, he's there. What I love about the man who makes the puppets is that he's also made these two other puppets—and there may be even more—of people who hang out in the park, people who most of us wouldn't notice. One of them is Doris, an older woman with gray hair, flower dress, gray sweater, old stockings. The puppet Doris is an exact replica of the living Doris. And he's also made another puppet—Wally, I think—a guy who's spent a lifetime on the street, too. I love what Sticks is mirroring back into the world. He's respecting these people and animating them in a way—so we can see them.

MK: Like theater, in a way. That's what I want when I go to the theatre—that idea of us mirrored back to us. I went to see The Apple Family cycle of plays by Richard Nelson being done a few years ago at the Public Theater. These are four plays about how political life intersects with private life and the action of each play is simply a group of people who gather around a table for a meal on the eve of the tenth anniversary of 9/11 or the 50th anniversary of JFK's assassination or Obama's election night. Each play opened on the actual night of the occasion being remembered. So, for instance, the last play, *Regular Singing*, opened on

November 22nd, 2013, JFK's anniversary.

The plays reminded me, in a way, of this experiment called the Dialogue Project, which was done at MIT. People spent time in a room and talked while they were being recorded. I know this because I used to transcribe some of the sessions. It was all sort of free fall—they would talk about their lives, of course, but eventually—because of the intimacy and the empathy that was coming out in these people by virtue of being in a group—the subject always seemed to go to world peace. That was what people really wanted to talk about. That was the subject under the story of their lives. Or maybe it was running parallel.

What's so fascinating about Nelson's plays is how they are about the physical, practical world we actually live in. In most works of art, there's a suspension of disbelief and nobody really talks about what they read, or what movies they see, or the real anything. Everyone seems to live in a world without ideas except for the ones they have in context to a kind of fiction. These Apple Family plays had real ideas and real things: like the Rainbow Room and Nixon or Bard College or Obama. It was like listening to an essay—the way the ideas were formulated.

MH: People don't eat in movies, either. Except Brad Pitt. He's always eating in the movies. In one of the *Ocean* movies—in virtually every scene—Brad Pitt is eating something. People never go to the bathroom in the movies either. Or you never see someone waiting for someone coming out of the bathroom.

MK: Or read. You almost never have a scene where someone enters a room and there's somebody sitting there reading. But there is that amazing scene in *Silence of the Lambs* where Hannibal Lecter is reading, of all things, an issue of *Poetry* magazine. There's a long shot on the cover—astonishing for a couple of reasons. It said as much about him as the killings did and supported the audience member who can't understand why they are fixated with a killer. And we don't see him kill anybody until—as it turns out—the scene after *Poetry* magazine.

MH: Have you read *Dirty Wars* by Jeremy Scahill? I just saw the documentary based on it—which was devastating. The next day I was walking my dog and passed the two delis I always pass and see the headlines in the *Post*, the *News,* and the *Times* about a drone strike in Afghanistan. And, after learning about these assassinations and drone strikes—and there have been hundreds of them—which is what Scahill's movie is about—so many civilians have been killed "by mistake."

The cover of the *Post* was gratuitous and gross—some horrible joke about a drone strike killing a wedding party, instead of a party they'd hoped to kill. There was no compassion in the report, which also said three terrorists might have been part of the wedding. And nobody knows if the bride and groom were killed. And that was it. I couldn't find anything about the bombing over the next two days in the news. We are asleep.

To live in this country at this time—to live in a first world country, which is what we are—to live in an empire that is waging war or has a military presence in seven countries—all of this is something very easy to forget. No one is talking about it in the media; no one is talking in mainstream media about the fact that many of us have what we have—our phones, and our cars, and our comforts—all this at the expense of other people. Even the Kennedy assassination—the relationship between Jack Ruby and Oswald and the CIA—and all these training camps, and who was trained by who—is still not common knowledge. It feels like we're just constantly going to sleep, while the government is saying, it's okay, it's okay, we'll take care of it.

So, art wakes people up and art revives people—like those plays that you're talking about—and like the puppeteer in Washington Square Park. It's art that reminds us that the political and the personal are deeply connected and that the public and the personal are connected. That was Adrienne Rich's entire project, wasn't it?

MK: Adrienne wrote: "The moment when a feeling enters the body is political."

MH: But, back then I thought, what in the world is she talking about? And I was in this class, thinking: how is this possible? Her book, *Diving Into the Wreck*, was a book that was too hard for me to read. I couldn't see it. It took me months and years to see what she was talking about.

MK: The amazing thing about Adrienne was how singular she was. Why aren't there more people like this? Was she so important and loved because she stood alone in the wilderness? Her readings would attract, sometimes, a thousand people.

MH: She was a global thinker, and I don't know that I am. I think about that a lot—people who can write from oneself, and see out—like Audre Lorde, Adrienne, or Muriel Rukeyser. These are people who can look out and see the whole world. Then, there are people who are more interior, but still have a huge effect, I think—like Paul Celan, or James Wright. Or Brenda Hillman, right now, who is such a lyrical, interior poet and who is also very political. It's a very interesting place to be—living inside the American empire at the beginning of the 21st century, the beginning of it—because I doubt that we'll be the empire for much longer. We really need to look at who we are and where we are.

We did this poetry event in Washington Square Park that was so exhilarating—a 20-minute, out loud, call-and-answer poetry kind of church which involves saying the words of another writer and using the human microphone from the Occupy Movement. It broke down the wall between the audience and the so-called speaker. No one is watching. That's the thing, right? Not to watch anymore?

But back to what you were saying about The Apple Family plays— the great plays are the ones where we don't feel we're watching but actually participating in some way.

MK: Marie Irene Fornes did this, literally, with her play *Fefu and Her Friends*. The audience was divided into four parts, and each one stood in a room on the stage and listened to someone speaking, and then moved to the next room, and the room after that. The genius was that it was written in such a way that no matter where somebody started, you were able to get the full experience. And the play always made sense. The very design of it gave the play a great sense of empathy.

MH: Empathy is the answer to everything, isn't it? Hundreds of people go to plays and not to poetry readings. I think we should stop calling poetry "Poetry." I think we should start saying, come to a performance about sex and death and doubt.

MK: Where we read poems.

MH: But don't tell anybody that. We have to begin to call it something else.

MK: So people will come.

MH: Why are The Apple Family plays completely sold out at the Public Theatre? Why is poetry still—except for people like Adrienne Rich or Billy Collins—who is another breakout poet for other reasons—so obscure? I think we have to answer that. And, we have to reframe it in the culture in a different way. Well, now that I think about it, performance poets are reframing it—hundreds of younger people go to hear and see performance people and rappers. Oh, it might be the page poets who need to recalibrate—not to give up the page—but add another way for poetry to be seen and heard.

MK: What does that reframing entail, do you think?

MH: People have tried to document what was happening in Washington Square Park, but it always looks like it's one person reading and that gets annoying, because it's not. It's everybody saying the poem at the same time. That experience is so different from listening to a poet.

When everybody says, "I sing the body electric" together it's really electric. And I'm not saying that every poetry reading should be like call and answer, but a way of putting it in a kind of context where there are no spectators.

MK: One of the great things about the musical *Hair* was that they put Shakespeare to music. "What a piece of work is man? How noble in reason . . . ." I'd never read Shakespeare before or couldn't care less about him. But when I heard him presented in a song, it was thrilling. And "I sing the body electric" was put to music in the movie *Fame*. Lynda Barry, the writer and cartoonist, reframes poetry, too. She says, if you take Frost's "Whose woods are these, I think I know, his house is in the village though," you can sing it to the tune of "Hernando's Hideaway" from the Broadway musical *The Pajama Game*.

MH: Yes. And there's Emily Dickinson and "The Yellow Rose of Texas." A lot of her poems go to that song.

MK: And you remember them. They get into your body and stay there. Speaking of Robert Frost, I know he's one of your influences in your own work. Who else is an influence, do you think?

MH: Seamus Heaney has been a big influence on me—especially his book *Seeing Things*. It's interesting, Robert Frost and Seamus Heaney. Who knew? I started reading Heaney's poems from the beginning—straight through. It's just fascinating to see the patterns and repetitions and the deepenings. He must say the words "I loved" dozens of times. I loved this, I loved that—it's one of the most common phrases he uses.

MK: Like Hikmet's *Things I Didn't Know I Loved*.

MH: Well, in a sense—but Hikmet has been in prison a long time—his tone is very different from Heaney's. Heaney is a celebrator of the earth and of tribal delights—as in *Seeing Things*, a childhood of brothers and sisters making games out of any old thing like a couch or a rope. It's been just wonderful to be in his company every day. And I was thinking, again, about the interior life.

We were talking about people saying poems together, out in public, and plays—where you don't feel like a watcher, but you're together with a whole lot of people—the way we used to go to the movies; where you would have a collective experience together—individual, but all together, which is so important.

And yet, every day, for maybe an hour or 45 minutes, I'll be just with Seamus. And it looks like I'm alone, but I'm reading him and it's totally interior. It's been so rich. I want more and more of my life to be two things: going out to theater and concerts and places where I am with people of my species, and also home, where I can actually inhabit the interior chambers of my own soul. So, poetry can be both. Which I think is what Adrienne was doing all along. She was an orator, in a way—a spokesperson in the world.

MK: One of the great things about seeing her read was how she engaged with the audience. And again—the fact that she was standing with people, not in front of them. She was a great reader of poems.

MH: Grace Paley was the same way. You always just felt that you were with Grace at eye level—and she was talking.

MK: Yes. Everything they said was all of a piece. I see a lot of people just sort of getting up there to present themselves. Show and tell. It feels sometimes like the work only belongs to them and that's why I think poetry gets a bad rap, because it's presented in a way where you need credentials to get into the club. And you don't. You just have to be a human—awake, listening.

MH: That was the gift of Jack Gilbert's poetry. He was so completely one soul who said that we can't give up delight. We always feel included in his work. You feel like he's talking with you all at the same time.

There's this amazing book, *Against the Pollution of The I* by Jacques Lusseyran—a man who was blinded at eight, who worked for the

Resistance in France and was turned in with a thousand other people and sent to Buchenwald. He writes so movingly about being in the camps. Of the thousand there, two survived and he was one of them. And he says, now I'm going to say a word that one cannot say, unless you've been there. There's joy, even in Buchenwald.

And he talked about a day when they were all in these freezing showers and there were a thousand men in a room that could only hold 30 people. They were wet and it was awful, and you couldn't move. And someone began to say a poem out loud, and everyone made space for this person. And Lusseyran wrote that they all felt as if they were being warmed by a hearth, as this person said the poem. And then another person said a poem. And then another person said a poem.

But these were not poems about loss. These were poems about bread and apples and sunlight—poems about the beauty of the world. That's what people wanted to hear. If anyone started to say a poem that wasn't about that beauty, they wouldn't listen. There it was, Gilbert's "We must risk delight."

Against the Pollution of the I is such a wonderful book. It is so moving. It opened up places in me I didn't know were there and reminded me of what's important. He talked about the gift of being blind and how sighted people are handicapped because they could actually believe that surfaces matter; that surfaces are the truth.

MK: What have you been reading lately aside from Heaney?

MH: Oddly enough, I've been reading Thomas Merton.

MK: The sacred or the secular stuff?

MH: *Zen and the Birds of Appetite*. I'm so late to reading this. But he writes about Meister Eckhart—who I love—and says that Eckhart was very close to being a Zen master. And what he's talking about is how he sees the presence of God and Zen's notion of emptiness and Meister Eckhart's notion of extreme poverty of spirit—giving up everything— even the idea of God. So that God can come and possess you. It's very similar to the Zen idea of the void or emptiness.

And then he talks about the church in the '60s—how the post-ec-umenical thinking—and one could sense this in the bad poetry and music of the time—had ceased to be representative of a church that was celebrating the presence of the divine. It had become a church that was encouraging a connection of the human community. People would get together and have a community—which was this hunger they had; make meals, do social work. But what was discouraged, oddly, was meditation and prayer and the notion of a presence of the divine.

And, as soon as I read it, I thought, my God, it's true. It became like a hootenanny—moving, because we're all together. He was talking about how the mystical essentially upends the authority of the church constantly. You can't have the structure of the church. The mystical doesn't pay attention to that; doesn't have anything to do with that. And that's where I was yesterday.

And then I was reading Seamus and his turf people. Actually, I've read to where he's just gotten married and it's very beautiful because he writes, within these limits, now, I have lived my life. He has that gorgeous poem—"Field of Vision"—about a woman in a wheelchair in a house in a country who sits in a doorway and looks out all day and how her view is made clearer by what bars the way. She can see deeper in, because of the frame around the door.

So, I'm very interested in the frame around things, these days. Being a mother is a door, is a frame. It's a limit, to an extent, because I have to be home. I make meals. I'm there when my daughter goes to bed. I'm there when she wakes up. I make her breakfast. And I've really come to love that limitation, if you will—that anchoring—that frame in life. It's new for me to understand that.

MK: Are you used to the new thinking—being a mother?

MH: Everything changes. And it sounds so corny—but now there's somebody I would die for. There's somebody I would put myself in front of a car for.

MK: Real love.

MH: All kinds of real love exist. Mother love is one kind—and as every mother knows it is joyful and it's not without its ambivalence.

MK: When you were the New York State Poet for two years, you staged a public artwork called "The Poet Is In." Could you talk about it a little bit?

MH: Yes. "The Poet Is In" was an interactive public art performance of a kind. It was a way to bring poetry to the public world, to the streets and public intersections where those who might not know poetry could access it, as well as people who already loved poetry could bump into it and be refreshed, moved, celebrated, and resuscitated. The model is inspired by the old *Peanuts* comic strip character Lucy who often sat at her booth with a sign that said "The Doctor Is In."

MK: Explain how it works—the logistics?

MH: It's a simple setup: A poet sits at a desk with a lamp, a typewriter, a bell, a timer, a stamp that says ORIGINAL, carbon paper, and white copy paper. Another chair is pulled to the desk, at an angle, for the person who wishes for a poem to sit and wait. The desk provides a space that is a refuge from the movement around them, a place for safety and repose. So, the Poet is there to write a poem for that person and spends a minute or two asking some questions, talking in general—that kind of thing. Getting to know them. After a few minutes of that, the Poet turns over the timer, and in three minutes writes a poem for that person—never worrying about mistakes. Mistakes happen on a typewriter, which is why we use one. The Poet puts XXXXs through the wrong word and types the necessary one. It is a great reminder that imperfections are human.

At the conclusion of writing she rings the bell, stamps the poem with the ORIGINAL stamp, signs and dates the poem, and pulls it out of the typewriter. Then, she signs the poem and reads it to the recipient before giving them the original. The carbon copy is kept in a box to archive.

When we first put on the event, it was at Grand Central Terminal in Vanderbilt Hall. We were just astonished at the response. Some people stood in line for over two hours to receive a poem. And when the Poet read the poem to the person who came for it, that person often wept. It was an utter joy.

MK: I love that you used a typewriter. I bet many young people didn't know what a typewriter was. Or carbon paper, for that matter.

MH: The kids were fascinated about how you could make a lot of mistakes—Xs and crossing words out. All the poems had all the "mistakes" in them.

MK: Like Mary Ruefle who said in a letter to me, "isn't it great how you have to cross out words to make sense?"

MH: Yes—and poetry is the place where the meaning is as much in the silence as it is in the words.

Lynda Barry

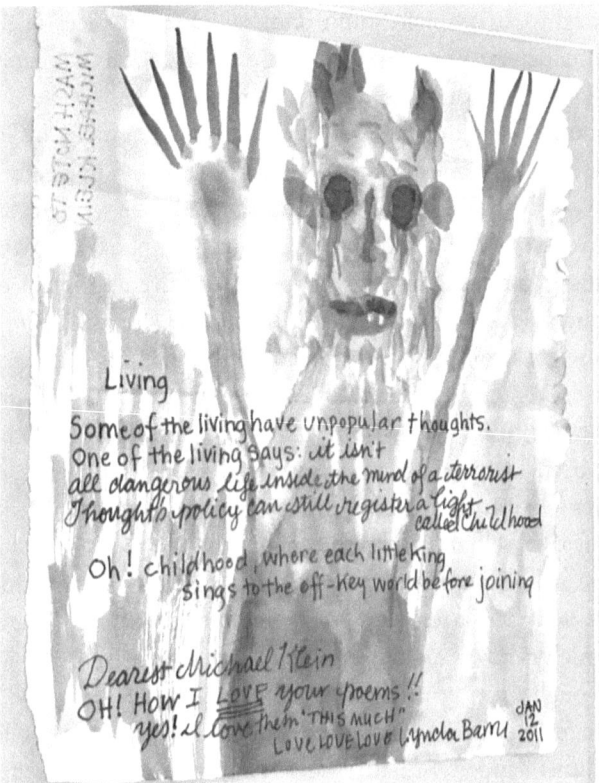

The image you are looking at is from the summer of 2011 when Lynda Barry was a visiting artist at Goddard College's low-residency MFA program. I like to think of this image as her illuminated reaction to a poem called "Living" from my second book, *then, we were still living*. She presented it to me one morning after day two of her gig—a gig she thought—in a hurried misreading of the offer letter—meant a one-week fellowship and not the two-day, give-a-reading-and-workshop-and-leave proposal we usually give writers who come to Vermont. We all wanted to hire her permanently, never mind kick her off campus after a week.

I knew *of* Lynda for years—the same way I know other writers by name or with the lingering curiosity that stops just short of actually making a point to get to their work. Besides, she was known mostly for being a cartoonist, and I'm not open enough to cartoons, in the same way I find it difficult to sit through an animated film—even when some of them happen to be brilliantly made. I always think of this great thing the playwright Christopher Shinn once said about movies in 3-D. I'm paraphrasing here: "When I'm watching a movie, I don't suddenly have a desire to have things on the screen get closer to me."

I watched everyone fall in love with Lynda that night at Goddard's iconic Haybarn Theater, her side-trips into music and poetry, and afterwards I began searching for everything she had ever written. How can you resist someone pointing out through impromptu song stylings that Robert Frost's "Stopping by Woods on a Snowy Evening" scans the same as "Hernando's Hideaway" from the musical, *The Pajama Game*: "Whose woods these are I think I know/His house is in the village, though" and "I know a dark, secluded place/a place where no one knows your face."

In the 71 years I have been, most of the time, a decent person, I have also been lucky to be around other persons whose very presence is so authentic and so surprising and so beyond most people that I lose sense of my own self and vanish momentarily into theirs. And I'm lucky that I've been able to hold people like this close enough to consider them friends, even if "close enough" stretches out over long distances and times—which is how I quickly came to know Lynda.

I thought, nearly instantly, that we would become good friends, stay in touch, maybe even share our work with each other, collaborate. But that didn't happen; or hasn't yet anyway. But every so often, Lynda's particular way of being has prompted me to try and get touch with her again, even though a message might never get read. In the end it doesn't matter. Her one act of startling generosity on a winter morning in Vermont is to me the very meaning of *enough*.

My Con Man, Mon Amour

That was the year the country installed a Disney creation in the White House the first time.

The year of hearing that we're living in a computer matrix.

The year of my money trouble and my husband's trouble with his Bipolar II diagnosis and the mind-mystery of how to find the correct calibration of drugs to keep him from cycling downward or thinking of suicide.

This was the year I found myself volunteering for a passion scam online—a scam, in the beginning, that felt the way all counterfeit love begins online—like great luck. I helped the narrative get written because I was falling for a stranger who, in addition to his handsomeness, was promising me his wild nature and generosity.

This was pre-pandemic.

I didn't have a name for what was happening to me, what I was succumbing to, not yet, not during the overture.

I left my body to go online and found him, rigging how it was going to play out—the true action behind his generous nature: the bait, the texts, the calls, the money. I didn't know what he was doing until I knew what he was doing. And even then, my mind, always lassoed by magical thinking, believed in the sincerity of attraction enough that it canceled out anything I found even remotely duplicitous.

I was a screen.

The only thing I knew for sure was that in the dizzy sunstroke of a crush, I didn't know how I was tricked into living a different life.

We found each other in the fall: body electric meeting body electric. Finding someone in the shine of virtual time and space had love/lust written all over it. I had waited for a long time to be made exactly like this: to be made of light. I'd been reading a lot of esoteric literature about how, in the fifth dimension, we become bodies of light, of psychic energy—bodies that can travel through time.

This was the year I couldn't perform my job or remember appointments, or dates I made with friends.

One day, at the beginning of this imaginary life, I got a phone call during a class I was teaching—my friend, Marie, wondering where I was, because we were supposed to be meeting for a movie 15 minutes ago. I remembered planning to see her, but I didn't remember confirming the date, which movie, which time.

It was a sundial year. The sundial turns time into a shadow across the length of itself—the year of everything happening at once. And happening badly.

And I was in something bad. But the badness felt vague because of the lust mixed up in it, singing louder than anything, like the hazy thinking that went with it. Which meant me sticking with it. Which meant that I thought the situation would somehow reverse and return to real promises. Or, that he would say it was all a joke, just to see how serious I was about all the silly, amorous, too-quickly-appearing feelings we kept dosing each other with in emails and texts and daily calls.

I stayed with it because I'd never been tricked like this before. And I couldn't make it make sense, because I had nothing to compare it to. From as far back as I can remember, I've always wanted to have something like an improvisatory life—which only meant, in my mind, being free. Never reckless.

I was arrogant to think something like that would never happen to me. I wasn't the kind of person something like this would happen to. But my allegiance to my own naivete was necessary—not only for the scam to succeed, but also for it to ultimately fail. My crime was revealing myself to an electronic ghost in the shape of someone handsome, a man with no debt. Which meant that my conman wasn't a complete cypher, except that he lied with every breath he took.

And, of course, the picture I saw of him was not the picture I saw later, when the jig was, as they say, up. And whatever generosity he had was in the time he spent making sure he could get as much money out of me as he could. And most of it was, as they say, money I didn't have. The money that I did have: magical thinking money: credit.

I needed help, but never asked for it, or didn't know who I could ask. I may have felt lustful, but I also felt ashamed to have reached a rabbit hole with such blind ambition. The one or two people I did tell parts of the story seemed more entertained by the whole thing than feeling it necessary to give me advice on how to stop jumping into the rabbit hole. Maybe they hadn't known me long enough to know what I considered actual IN TROUBLE.

And there I was.

And there I stayed for months: IN TROUBLE.

I kept disappearing into trouble.

It kept happening to me, but in a sense, I wasn't there.

I suffered every moment it happened and was ecstatic for every moment it was happening. I was finally able to have places in my body where two kinds of sensation happened at once. The lower part of my body was in ecstasy and the rest of what I vaguely identified as myself was suffering.

I suffered the air I was breathing.

I wasn't in sync with what I looked like.

I was confused when I looked into a mirror, the face looking back in constant judgment.

I was eating, but not very much, because my mind was starving for something rational.

I didn't always remember to take a shower.

I didn't get the mail.

I wasn't connected to people, except to the one person I found online and who found me.

We were living virtually, but we were living in the blunt truth of never seeing each other, knowing we would never see each other, which of course was essential—the nevers—if the scam was going to fly.

The Geologist's Dream

That was the year, the late summer, that I met a geologist online who preposterously called himself Clive Owen ("Oh c'mon, that's an actor." "Okay," he said. "Clive Owen Simpson"). He was a geologist. His job was to bring something up from the Earth. That's how he phrased it: *something up from the Earth.*

You don't actually meet people online, you *find* them there—if they're ready to lustfully pounce—standing at an imaginary river, reeling someone in. How did I become one of those crazy Americans invested in the lie that finding love online was divine intervention?

Of course, Clive Owen Simpson didn't exist. And by the time I figured out what was really happening, I wondered who this person was in the real world and where he was and who I was in the real world and where I was. All of a piece. All of a transmission. What was going to happen after all the money went and I had no hope of finding him to get it back?

It was about the money, and it wasn't about the money.

I disappeared with Clive Owen Simpson into a geologist's dream of capturing, capturing me, because nothing about it was true except the unidentifiable accent—a strange British/Swedish mix. That and I had a phone number to a phone he answered. But where was he calling from? Where was I calling to?

His power over me: he was the only one of us who knew where we were.

So, if Clive Owens Simpson said he's calling from Alaska, Alaska was where he was calling from. He could be in Congo or Brussels or Beirut, or around the corner, but Alaska was the name for the place he was calling from. There's nothing in the margins of reality that says you can't switch any two names around.

Clive Owens Simpson is a geologist who works in the field, not a petty thief moving through the world on the waves of money he made from other scams.

After Alaska, he was calling from Canada. Then later, when the real nature of the relationship became morbidly clear, London. London was where he said he was settling his dead father's affairs and needed $20,000 to pay the estate attorneys. And where, when I called the manager of the hotel he'd been living in for a week so I could pay the bill, I distinctly heard chickens squawking in the background—CHICKENS—to which one of the many friends who was getting my brief reports about my experience reacted by saying: "He wasn't in London. He was in Nigeria. You're in love with a Nigerian with AIDS."

Clive Owens Simpson said he lived, when he wasn't pretending to be somewhere else, in New York, on Central Park West, in the same building Barbara Streisand used to live, which I knew because I lived on Central Park West as a kid and I would see her coming out of her building with her dog.

The day after we found each other online, I went to his building, while he was in "Canada," and asked the staff of doormen if there was a Clive Owen Simpson living there. "No," said the three gatekeepers. I called Clive and asked what was going on. And after he yelled at me for not trusting him, he told me that the doormen (how could I not think of this?) were instructed not to say anything to anybody about his living there. And if that wasn't enough to locate my injured life in Suspicion Village, the end of the conversation went:

MK: Where are you, by the way? You sound like you're in a tunnel with piccolo players.

COS: In Montreal, at a bar. I left New York this morning.

Leaving town—I found out later in my research on how online scams work—is how the conman is sure to keep enough distance between him and his mark.

Dark Geology

I was lost in the waiting for something—for an answer to my last text or email—every one of mine to him ending with a type of wronged faith: *When are we finally going to meet?* And each time he was reminded of how he'd promised we would, he backed off just a little, though not enough to stop his trap from springing down on my money. Online scammers, I found out later, take as much as they can as long as they can, while the mark is convinced real love is still doing the driving.

Drifting—the opposite of magnetism—became a theme to the magnetism anyway.

In the drift, I lost things.

I lost time, which was how this trauma came to be known.

I lost my house keys on more than three occasions. Once, only an hour after parking my car in Provincetown, I realized I'd lost the key, only to find it when somebody rested it carefully on the door handle.

I lost money. A lot of money. Money, like a gambler's money is lost, like all the money I didn't have. Play money. Credit money. Wire money. Advance money. Borrowed money.

I actually borrowed money so I could lose it—like a garden variety drunk drowning in debt at the races. I was a drunk, but I had stopped drinking. And at this point, I couldn't even remember what sobriety felt like, except when it came on like a ghost light, barely filling in the outlines of an empty stage.

This worst thing I ever did might have been a side effect of my new medication—antidepressants, after the election. I didn't get out of bed for three days because I didn't know what to do with time, as long as an entire day.

I couldn't structure my mind around a president who kept ghosting the country.

Ghosting the world.

Ghosting anybody who wasn't white. Ghosting the English language in his speeches.

Ghosting the economy.

Was the truth a side effect of life, or was the lie?

The only side effect I had was more depression and stranger behavior. I was a stranger in my own body, acting out stranger behavior. I didn't bother to look up the possible effects of my drugs because I don't usually experience side effects—just a drug doing what it's supposed to do. Everything I did to abuse my body in my 20s and 30s must have galvanized the electric lining between my body and soul.

People always say I don't look my age. And when they tell me how young I look, I tell them it's the laughter following me wherever I go. That and I'm pickled in alcohol. I'm preserved.

Hour of the Wolf

I once lived in a white colonial whose shutters kept blowing loose during bad weather, causing them to bang against the house. The sound scared my brother, but I told him to just listen, because eventually the sound of the weather and its banging would fall to a soothing rhythm, which it always would just as we were almost asleep.

One of our bedroom windows led onto the roof, and on clear nights, I'd open it and walk as close to the edge as I could without falling—not to conquer anything like a fear of falling—but to register the feeling of risk.

Risk is extra life.

I once took a branch from a nearby tree and stuck it into the gas tank of my father's Triumph and licked the stick afterwards. I wanted to know if the intoxicating smell of gasoline was what it tasted like, too. How did I live after that? How did I not consider how dangerous that was? Is there any amount of gasoline someone could ingest before it killed them?

I'm certain this happened, the way I just remembered it. But I also know memory is inaccurate and imaginative, and I can't bring back the taste of gasoline.

I don't know why I never told anyone about the gas or why I never panicked afterwards—the same way I'll never know why an actor named Sterling Holloway from the old TV series, *The Life of Riley*, found my bedroom one winter night and stood naked in a darkened corner with devil-like horns shooting from his head. The horns were wet and glistened like teeth. I was too paralyzed to speak and couldn't rationalize him as anything like an hallucination, which at that age, was a phenomenon I had never experienced.

I was awake, though. I know I wasn't dreaming. And I did come back to myself through the terror with a scream that got my mother to throw open the door and throw on the light. Funny thing about that light. It somehow transformed the whole of Sterling Holloway into only his face, imprinting itself slowly on the ceiling, until the shadow-face was finished, making a stain that never went away and that nobody saw except me.

These early experiences, being a daredevil on the roof or bearing witness to the strange, could make me momentarily forget who I was, which, in its way, lessened my fear. In that subtle slip of forgetting, I found my imagination. Which, of course, was how Sterling Holloway got conjured to begin with.

Years later, when I started my close reading of alcohol, it wasn't the booze that was making me forget who I was, it was the danger of not knowing what could happen. Addiction, my addiction, was wired for danger and drew me into a lifetime of long odds where I somehow made it out alive.

How many times did I pray to God when I was drinking to keep me out of danger—always promising, *this is it, God ... the last drink*. All the while knowing it was only the last drink before the next drink, which was the drink I wanted the most—the one up ahead, the one that hadn't been poured yet—and then poured, without end, into the rest of my life.

Considering how dangerous everything is, nothing is very frightening.

When I met Clive Owen Simpson, I recognized that, even with more than 30 years sober, there was still a helix of danger mixed into my DNA. And now, I knew the cost of it. And yet, here I was again, so many years later—adult years and not the wonder years of nothing-very-frightening—entering that hot zone of men—queer or heterosexual—preying on older queer men who act lonely in public.

What It's Like to Stand Next to Him

His first email. His picture. The picture of his cock.

His nonsensically romantic texts and phone calls.

You have to fall in love in a hurry in the virtual world, to be certain love, and he, actually exist. But you also have to know what it feels like to stand next to him to affirm that your pheromones are a match—and this can never happen. He will only and forever be a figment of your imagination.

I knew—though he promised to get me out of considerable debt—that there was never going to be a me retired and owning nothing to anybody.

There was no Range Rover, the one he promised to give me if I could get to his house in Malibu that didn't exist and drive it back to New York, which did exist because I lived there.

Everything he said or did was acting. I once told a friend after I broke up with an actor (and not the first actor either), that actors tend to cast themselves in each of their relationships without ever stepping outside their role of being in a relationship. They can never just be the person they are, apart from the performance, when they're alone in the dressing room, after the play, handing the costume to the dresser.

Begin Again

I was, during the sultry summer of being interrupted badly by the internet, living alone in New York. And even though ours had been a mostly loving, healthy-ish relationship for 15 years, my husband was living in Provincetown, where his Bipolar-II disorder made him crazy, floundering in the wake of two failed businesses that lost large amounts of money. We separated, in part, because his behavior and my loss at how to live with his self-abuse and the verbal abuse he gave me had reached a point where I thought we would have to break up.

After the loneliness of that, of still loving him, but not knowing how to live with still loving him, coupled with the loneliness every native New Yorker feels when they live in a sprawling metropolis, eventually pushed me online in search of an answer in the cliché of finding someone out there to love.

There's an effective shiver in loneliness that convinces you somehow that living is theoretical and not held strongly enough by its own beauty. And the internet, in a lot of ways, flattens life out, not into theory, per se, but into a keener awareness of being held in real time. But faster. Being virtual is the browsing eye standing in for the body electric.

So, as I've said, my body fell away
into a body called Clive.

But my body wasn't floating outside my body—the way it can thin out into spirit that stares down from a height at the body it looks down upon—the body, the spirit sailed out of in the extreme light aimed at the operating table. I could feel a slow unpeeling, a separation from self. And often, pleasurably, like the sunburn that turns you briefly into another person.

This existential *what happened* became a six-month period of acting in love, and dread. And when it finally ended, I was traumatized and broke, on the verge of ending my marriage.

The danger and my call to performance were delivered as a love thing
and then a money thing
and from the start, (I didn't know this) a criminal thing.

But to say a love thing or a money thing isn't being realistic. My surrender to our telephone calls and texting and my role as a willing accomplice in a cybercrime ended in a psychic pain I thought would never be cured. I had shocked and terrified myself by "falling in love" with a stranger in order to stumble out of a crippling loneliness brought on by the election and by being separated from my husband—who, as it happens—I met/I found—the same way Clive Owen Simpson found me—online, in a virtual waiting room, until another one enters, and you somehow are able to recognize someone you've never seen before.

The Book of Names

I managed to make it the block and a half to the gas station for cigarettes, but I wasn't too sure about walking back home. I was still a little wobbly since the knee had only been replaced that Tuesday. So, I got an Uber after the cigarettes and told the driver to please give me a minute to get into his car, I've just had surgery.

"Of course," he said.

And of course he said of course. Because as I'd soon learn he'd gotten a new knee himself. He knew how it was. What if we could live in a world where people knew—no matter what kind of person crossed their path—*how it was?*

"But what made you come out of the house?"

"I smoke," I said.

He then went into the old saw about smoking and its richly varied horrors, adding, "You'll save money, too," his plea I should quit.

"Addicts don't care about how much the drugs cost," I told him.

He said, "You should pray to get your addiction stopped. Pray to have the next cigarette you smoke taste like shit."

That settled me, in a way, the stranger sitting up front, Paul, as he became known, looking out for me. Paul wasn't preachy or brainwashed. His words came through with an assuring wave of humility. An islander, I thought.

As I was about to get out of the car, I noticed an open journal of handwritten notes wedged between his seat and where I was sitting.

"I don't know if this is yours or maybe a fare left it," I said, handing it to him.

The word "fare" felt odd, as it was leaving my mouth, but I also call a refrigerator an "icebox" most of the time.

"Thank you," he said. "That's my book of prayers."

"What kind of prayers?" I asked him.

"Prayers for people I've picked up that could use some help. I could put your name down if you want."

"Please do, I said, "that would be great."

I wanted to say, *please do, I could really use some prayers*, but didn't want to sound like anybody but myself at that particular moment.

And as I watched him add my name to the others, which I imagined nightly filled his book of prayers, I was struck by the same thought I get when I'm inside moments that feel ordained—a little outside life—similarly lit like this moment.

The thought: I can be happy now with just this one and only.

Just this.

At last, I found the man with the book.